Memphis **BLUES**

Birthplace of a Music Tradition

Memphis *BLUES*

BIRTHPLACE OF A
MUSIC TRADITION

William Bearden
Foreword by Knox Phillips

ARCADIA
PUBLISHING

Published by Arcadia Publishing
Charleston SC, Chicago IL, Portsmouth NH, San Francisco CA

Printed in the United States of America

Library of Congress Catalog Card Number: 2005935860

For all general information contact Arcadia Publishing at:
Telephone 843-853-2070
Fax 843-853-0044
E-mail sales@arcadiapublishing.com
For customer service and orders:
Toll-Free 1-888-313-2665

Visit us on the Internet at www.arcadiapublishing.com

CONTENTS

FOREWORD

In the late 1940s and early 1950s, the migration of African Americans out of the Mississippi Delta brought any number of talented and ambitious blues musicians to Memphis, where jobs were more plentiful, and the possibility of a better life was a realistic goal. In this fertile climate, for the first time their dreams of making it seemed more than just pipe dreams.

It was to help some of those aspiring musicians that my father, Sam Phillips, first opened his tiny recording studio at 706 Union Avenue, the Memphis Recording Service, in January of 1950, with the avowed purpose of making records "with some of those great black artists," as he said, "who just had no other place to go." He did this, as he often stated, at the risk of a good radio job, at the risk of his health, and at the risk of his young family's future—given the racially charged atmosphere of the time. He did it because of his belief in the music, in the musicians, and in the possibilities that Memphis (and America) had to offer. I always felt that the foundations for the musical contribution that Memphis would make to our world were laid with that original "revolution of hope"—hope in the sense that frustrated, creative, poor people had a place to go, be heard, be themselves musically no matter what that self might be. My father's mission was to give voice to those who had no voice.

Sam Phillips is probably best known for his discovery of Elvis Presley, Carl Perkins, Johnny Cash, and Jerry Lee Lewis, but he was no less proud—and that's an understatement—of his involvement with great blues musicians like B. B. King, Howlin' Wolf, Rufus Thomas, Little Milton, and Ike Turner, all at the earliest formative stages of their careers. I can only imagine the first time Sam listened and talked with a young, unknown B. B. King or Howlin' Wolf, no more than local radio personalities at the time, and convinced them that he wanted to record the music that meant the most to them. "I knew the sound I had heard in the cotton fields growing up," Phillips said later in life, "and I also knew that had I not tried to captured it, I would have been the biggest damn coward that God ever put on this earth." There was nothing that told the truth, Phillips said, more than gutbucket blues, and even if the white world may not have known it at the time, every one of those artists had something special that was almost bursting to get out. It was the beginning of Memphis's musical self-expression, what my father always prized as "self-expression in the extreme." It was the beginning of the "Memphis Sound," the Memphis music story. Which at its core is the story of people—black people and white people—working together.

That legacy of talented people coming together from diverse backgrounds is still the Memphis music story. Every day in studios across Memphis and in the clubs on Beale Street, songs are being written and recorded, records released, and music is being heard by the millions of tourists who come here to experience a little taste of this thing called the blues. But it's more than just blues music; it is the culture, the traditions, and the way of life here in Memphis. It's a feeling. We who live here and love it can't define just what it is, but if you let go and become a part of it, you can feel it.

Enjoy this walk through the Delta and Memphis and feel the power of the music that changed the world.

—Knox Phillips

ACKNOWLEDGMENTS

A Google search turns up 54 million Web sites with reference to blues music. It's mind-boggling when you think that just over 40 years ago, blacks and whites couldn't legally congregate in the same clubs. Things have changed. We now have the clarity of hindsight and context. When I initially thought about putting this book together, I somehow thought it would be easy. You see, I suffer from the optimism and exuberance of one who is, in Minnie Pearl's words, "just so proud to be here." I have the enviable job of packaging information and explaining things to people who have little or no knowledge of them. In my work as a filmmaker, I have created documentaries and museum exhibits on subjects as diverse as the Memphis cotton market, Gulf coast lighthouses, Renaissance art, the Mississippi River, cigars, Alzheimer's disease, historical cemeteries, urban parks, the Mississippi Delta, 1960s garage bands, and the art of the snowcone. I am fortunate to possess the curiosity of a librarian, the ability to look through thousands of photographs without going bonkers, and the moxie to believe that I can do it all with a flair that will resonate with my audience. I have listened to, read about, followed, debated, and discussed Memphis blues for over 35 years, but the single item that might come closest to qualifying me for this task is this: in my hometown of Rolling Fork, Mississippi, there was a juke joint called the Gold Coast. This club was originally a shotgun shack not unlike the rest of the houses on Blue Front, the street facing the Illinois Central railroad tracks, and home to a large population of African Americans who worked on the plantations, in the cotton gins and warehouses, and as domestics in the homes of the local whites. As a small child in the mid-1950s, I would sneak away from my backyard and walk the hundred yards or so to the back of the Gold Coast and, leaning against the building, feel the deep thunder of the bass and the driving of the kick drum course through my body. This experience, along with the music we heard in the cafés and shoe repair shops, sent me on a lifelong journey, not searching for the blues, but approaching the world with the blues in my pocket. I thank those nameless musicians, those people who dropped nickels in the jukeboxes, and those who lived the Delta life. My most sincere thanks and appreciation is offered to you.

Projects such as this could never be completed if it were not for the generosity of the conservators, writers, musicians, and photographers who populate the world of Memphis music. Help, clarification, and other greatly needed assistance have come from many quarters, and I have had the great pleasure of spending hours with some of the giants of Memphis music. The public archives of the Memphis Room at the Benjamin Hooks Public Library in Memphis and Special Collections of the University of Memphis Library are essential to the research and access to images that make a project such as this possible. I also want to thank the many scholars who have unearthed the truth, debunked the legends, and scoured the sidewalks of Memphis and the dusty backroads of the Delta in search of the blues. We are all in their debt.

Sid Selvidge has been so open, available, and accommodating during this process that I owe him a tremendous debt of gratitude. He has been at the forefront of Memphis music for over four decades, participating in some of the most significant events in our history. Today he is the producer and executive director of the internationally syndicated *Beale Street Caravan* and continues to record and perform. Dr. Doug Cupples, one of the world's foremost Civil

War scholars, was part of the "rediscovery" of the blues in the late 1960s. His insight and historical perspective have been essential to my understanding of this vast and rich subject. Judy Peiser is the co-founder of the Memphis-based Center for Southern Folklore. She has been an indefatigable chronicler and champion of the music and culture of Memphis and the South. The center's groundbreaking work in oral histories, films, photography, art, and music set the mark and paved the way for much of today's formalized study of the South. Steve Roberts is a gifted working photographer, specializing in music, whose goodness as a person is reflected back in the faces of his subjects. He recognizes that great photographs come from within. I spent a very enjoyable afternoon in the office of University of Memphis ethnomusicologist Dr. David Evans. He shared photographs and told stories of a time when very few people had an appreciation of the blues. His research, playing, and writing about the blues have added greatly to our knowledge and understanding of this music and culture. What can I say about Tater Red? He is simply the personification of the blues. Hailing from Ruleville, Mississippi, he has made the world richer by hosting the longest-running blues show on Memphis radio, creating unique works of Delta art, and manning the counter at the most important stop on Beale Street. If you don't know Tater Red, you're in for a treat. Executive director of the Blues Foundation Jay Seileman is a tireless and inventive advocate for the blues, a friend to blues lovers everywhere, and a good friend to me. David Less is a Memphis-born blues scholar who has led the Blues Foundation, has written for national magazines, and is the founder of Memphis International Records. His guidance has been both welcomed and essential. Howard Stovall, a longtime friend and colleague, was born on the plantation where Muddy Waters was first "discovered" and recorded. After having led the Blues Foundation for eight years, he now is the managing partner in Resource Entertainment Group, one the South's premier talent agencies. And then there's Don Nix: bluesman, songwriter, photographer, author, and "rememberer" of everything. The Memphis music scene would look very different indeed if Don Nix had not been around. His generous spirit and deep knowledge make him the ultimate Memphis treasure. Knox Phillips is a member of Memphis's first family of music. Throughout his long career, he has been a producer, publisher, label owner, and every other job one can hold in the music business. But it has been his commitment and dedication to the Memphis music and film communities that have defined him as the generous, unique, and talented person he is today. It is my pleasure to be his friend.

Each of the folks mentioned above has spent hours with me answering countless questions, loaning photographs (many previously unpublished), and generally helped shape my thinking about Memphis blues. My greatest wish is to get them all in one room together for the ultimate blues summit. Short of that event, I want to thank each of them for their assistance and guidance. As always, I want to thank the unknown photographers who captured these important moments and contributed their photographs to public archives. For reasons ranging from inspiration, friendship, encouragement, admiration, and a thousand other accolades, I want to thank the following people: Tom Bollard, Rae Nell Hunter, Tom Harris, Dudley Davis, Grace Young, Jay Martin, Wiley Brown, Marshall Jones, Robin Salant, David Nester, Calvin Turley, Bob Sekinger, Richard Johnston, Betsie Crawford, Mary Battle, Rafe Murray, Ernest Withers, Lauren Hesse, Changzhi Yu, Joe Whitmer, Percy Brown, Wesley Smith, Eddie Dattel, Keith Soltys, Peter Guralnick, Shelby Foote, Dick Raichelson, Paul Averwater, Jim Spake, Niko Lyras, Mike Taylor, Kevin Kane, Sam Tibbs, Pat Mitchell, Chuck Porter, Earnest Williamson, Kurt Clayton, Dave Smith, Ron Michael Hughes, Clark Secoy, Robert Waldon, David Durrett, Robert Beaver, Jerry Lambert, Keith Carmack, the GrayHounds, Leigh Ann and Mike Barns, Bill Robison, Hal Harmon, Ron Hall, Arthur Bell, Ken DeCell, Roger Truesdale, Charles Weissinger, Nick Secoy, Adam Secoy, David Spencer, the Goldcoasters, Bob Caldwell, Sam Phillips, Muddy Waters, Rufus Thomas, David Tankersley, Robert Gordon, Cato Walker, Greg Johnson, Marvell Thomas, Lori Finta, Maggie Bullwinkel, Jon Hornyak, Katherine Sage, Doug and Mandy McMinn, Don McMinn, Gary Phillips, Bob Friedstand, Carson Lamm, Rum Boogie Café, Ed Frank, Chris Ratliff, Jim Johnson, Patricia LaPointe, Emily Weaver, Luther Brown,

Greg Newby, Patrick Reilly, Paul Benjamin, Chuck's in Rolling Fork, Mildred Jones, Rollin Riggs, REG Entertainment, People's Pool Hall on Beale Street, Virginia Trigleth, and Cheryl, Savannah, Matt, and Maggie Bearden.

Author William Bearden grew up in the deep Delta town of Rolling Fork, Mississippi, the land where blues truly began. He is also the author of *Overton Park* and *Cotton: From Southern Fields to the Memphis Market*.

INTRODUCTION

In September 1991, I was in downtown Memphis sitting on the grass of Court Square listening to Memphis legend Jim Dickinson, his teenaged sons Cody and Luther, and Jim Spake romp through an eclectic set of blues, soul, and country music. They were performing as a part of the Center for Southern Folklore's annual Memphis Music Heritage Festival. My three-year-old son, Matt, was sitting in my lap, and as the band began the next song (they couldn't have been more than four bars into the intro), Matt turned to me, smiling, and quietly said, "Got My Mojo Working." Now that may not be a defining moment for most parents, but I felt a warm glow come over me, and it was as if he'd just scored the winning touchdown, made the double play, blocked the winning shot in a soccer match, or walked across the stage at graduation as class valedictorian; my three-year-old just identified a Muddy Waters song in under five seconds. This is most certainly behavior and personal aspirations that would make a Baptist cringe, but somehow I felt a measure of accomplishment that gave me an enormous sense of joy. In the land of blues, we are all pilgrims.

It has been said that blues is a big room. I say that blues is a big house with many rooms: closets, ballrooms, hidden nooks and crannies, formal sitting rooms, bathrooms, basements, attics, and little ramshackle lean-to additions built all around, not to mention the woodsheds and garages that occupy the backyard. To take this illustration to the next level, it could be said that the driveway of the this "blues house" is crowded with mules, tractors, a 1932 Ford coupe, a 1958 Lincoln, a 1962 Cadillac, a 1968 Volkswagen micro bus, a sleek $400,000 tour bus, a Ford Econoline van, several black limos, and a white Rolls-Royce.

This vision of the blues is nowhere more evident than at the annual W. C. Handy Blues Awards show held in Memphis each May. Although for almost a quarter century the show was a formal awards presentation with five or six performances, for the past two years, it has been the very embodiment of the state of the blues today. There in one long evening, one can see and hear the complete spectrum of the blues. With 30-plus acts ranging from Mississippi nonagenarian Robert Lockwood Jr. to young West Coast guitar slinger Kirk Fletcher, the story of the blues rolls over the audience like an unstoppable wave that has its origins in the field hollers and tiny churches of the Mississippi Delta 100 years ago. It is nearly overwhelming to be confronted with the breadth and depth of this natural force that we call the blues all under one roof in one night. Although I used to scoff at the fact that blues was being practiced by folks from outside the South, I have come to embrace and appreciate the fact that blues and its accompanying culture has spread to the far corners of the earth. To place boundaries of time, place, and skin color on the blues is to deny its power and importance. It has been my honor and pleasure to produce that show since 1998, a child's murky and ill-defined dream realized amid the rush of a big show; the lights and cameras and amplifiers and guitars, the backstage announcer, TelePrompTer, video playback, stage manager, interns, and trophy girls, artists, managers, piano tuners, roadies, hangers-on, photographers, and the ubiquitous "important people" who forever populate the backstage and exclusive receptions. This swirl of music and humanity has an almost calming effect on me as I slog my way through the chaos of the evening. Walking to my car after the show, usually at four o'clock in the morning, a quiet tranquility and a sense of accomplishment set in, and I feel as if I'm a link in the chain that has been unbroken since the first bluesman moaned his lament of lost love. I celebrate the change that has come about in our country and in the world that allows, without the fear of retribution, black and white people to be a part of this thing we call the blues.

I don't know how to tell a story without going to the well of my person experience and telling it through my eyes and ears. That is probably a deficiency or shortcoming on my part, but I simply do not possess the impartial approach or method of a scholar. There are mountains of scholarly research and opinion about this thing called blues. The study of blues has gained a status and a significance that would have been mind-boggling or, better yet, scoffed at by the likes of Muddy Waters or Howlin' Wolf. This is where the clear line of demarcation exists. There are those who have lived it and those who have studied it. Both are essential to its growth and success. Nearly all these distinctions and ground rules about who and what are the blues have come from scholars. I have encountered an enormous amount of ownership when it comes to the blues, yet in the end, it is owned by none of us but continues to be reshaped and redefined by those young musicians who come to the blues in ever-increasing numbers. I doubt that any musician about to pocket $65 for a recording session ever said, "Oh, gosh, that's a blues song and, alas, I'm a practitioner of the Memphis Soul genre." The blues has been poked and prodded, codified, dissected, argued over, term-papered, and seminared to death. There have been positions staked-out and defended over long-ago and minute happenings that have severed friendships and produce enmity still today. To the players, the lines are blurry, and they rarely tend to snub music that rubs shoulders with blues. Rufus Thomas, the originator of Memphis funk, sang the country music classic, "Today I Started Loving You Again" alongside "Did You Ever Love a Woman" and "Walkin' the Dog" in virtually every show he performed. It was music from the heart and music that spoke to him on that deepest level that he wanted to share with his audience, whether they were aficionados or simply getting their first taste. It is this musical schizophrenia that is evident across the landscape of Memphis music. It had its initial and most powerful occurrence on Elvis Presley's first record, that fateful convergence of the young hillbilly cat with visionary Sam Phillips and musicians Scotty Moore and Bill Black. On one side is the blues number "That's Alright Mama" followed by the bluegrass song "Blue Moon of Kentucky," and it worked. It worked so well in fact that it created a new genre of music: rock and roll. For that reason, I have cast a wide net in gathering images and stories for this book. The blues is indeed a big house.

Times have changed. In today's world it is possible to earn a college degree in the blues. It is also possible to take a field trip to a Mississippi juke joint. It is possible to hire a car to go on a pilgrimage of Memphis and Mississippi Delta blues sites. There are blues museums in towns like Clarksdale, Leland, and Greenwood, and more on the way. Although it may seem to some the height of commercialism, over-exposure or even exploitation, this is a good thing. It took people from outside the South to show us the importance of our indigenous music, and we were slow to recognize the obvious, partly because of the difficulties between the races and partly due to the fact that it was always here in front of us, not that strange and magical gift from an equally strange and far-off place, accessible only through rare little discs of vinyl. The assortment of explorers reads like a who's who of literary and musical royalty: Alan Lomax, Sam Charters, the Rolling Stones, Led Zeppelin, Eric Clapton, John Mayall, John Fahey, Bill Barth, Peter Guralnick, and dozens of others who scoured the record shops in New York, Boston, Chicago, London, and Liverpool, hungry for the strange sounds that stirred the soul and captured the imagination.

The blues is not safe. It is the boiling-over of emotions rubbed raw by injustice, inequality, and, most importantly, the power of love and jealousy that make a man do foolish things. The blues is bawdy. In 1978, we got Hollandale, Mississippi, bluesman Sam Chatmon to sing at a little festival in my hometown of Rolling Fork. By the third song, most of the white ladies of the audience were long gone. Sam had begun to do what he did best . . . sing about the many attributes and pleasures of women. And sing in graphic detail he did. It was a lesson in the blues

Blues is NOT safe.

that was not lost on me and my friends in the audience. I was somehow comforted by the fact that Sam did not tailor his performance to the crowd. He did not refrain from the frank and honest experiences of his long life. He was singing his blues. In this world of safe endeavors and moral guardrails, from Disney World to network television, it is good to know that some people operate on the outer edge, not caring about convention or political correctness. That is the legacy of the blues. Sam is long gone (he died in 1983), but that spirit of honesty still shines through in the writing and performing of modern bluesmen.

Since the mid-1980s, Beale Street is jumping again though in a different style and approach from its heyday. The clubs and bars have been around long enough to have served a couple of generations and therefore establish their identities in the minds and experience of millions of visitors. They have experienced the blues on Beale Street. The state of the blues today is also evidenced by the hundreds of bands from every corner of the United States and many foreign countries who enter the Blues Foundation–sponsored International Blues Challenge each January. For three days, the clubs on Beale Street are crowded with blues lovers of every stripe, intent on hearing the best that amateur blues has to offer. The winners go on to perform on the Handy Awards show in May. It is the natural way in Memphis, yet it is our greatest export. This deep feeling that was born in the Delta, born of hardship and drudgery, pain and wide-open joy, continues to resonate with people from the world over, people who want to touch and possess that attitude, that feeling, that thing called the blues.

—William Bearden
November 2005

Here is Memphis music royalty. In this 1999 photograph, Sam Phillips (left), the widely acknowledged "Father of Rock and Roll" and greatest producer of Memphis music, shows his love for Sun Records artist and rock and roll originator Jerry Lee Lewis (center) as Knox Phillips looks on in amusement. A successful producer in his own right, Knox has carried on the Phillips family tradition of innovation and dedication to the Memphis music community.

One

In the Beginning

This illustration from the 1860s tells it all. The enslavement of millions of African Americans is the greatest moral stain on the America story. But the combination of the two cultures has served to make the resulting culture admired and emulated around the world. (American Memory Collection.)

THE COLORED VOLUNTEERS.

Fremont told us, when this war was first begun,
How to save this Union, and the way it should be done,
But Kentucky swore so hard, and old Abe he had his fears,
So that's what's the matter with the Colored Volunteers.

CHORUS.— Give us a flag all free without a slave,
We will fight to defend it as our fathers did so brave
Onward boys, onward, it's the year of jubilee,
God bless America, the land of liberty.

Little Mack went to Richmond with three hundred thousand brave—
Said keep back the negroes and the Union he would save ;
But Mack he was defeated, and the Union now in tears,
Is calling for the help of the Colored Volunteers.

CHORUS.—Give us a flag all free without a slave, &c.

Old Jeff he says he'll hang us if we dare to meet him armed—
It's a very big thing, but we are not at all alarmed :
He has first got to catch us before the way is clear,
And that's what's the matter with the Colored Volunteers.

CHORUS.—Give us a flag all free without a slave, &c.

Here's to the gallant Fourth which has not yet been tried,
They are willing and are ready with their brothers to divide;
General Birney leads us on, so we have no right to fear,
And that is the making of the Colored Volunteers.

CHORUS.—Give us a flag all free without a slave, &c.

500 Illustrated Ballads, lithographed and printed by
CHARLES MAGNU", No. 12 Frankfort Street, New York.
Branch Office · No. 520 7th St., Washington, D. C.

Thousands of black volunteers joined in the fight for abolishment of slavery and the preservation of the Union during the Civil War. "Give us a flag all free without a slave," was the chorus of this anthem of the Union army volunteers. Lincoln signed the Emancipation Proclamation in 1864, setting the stage for over 100 years of struggle for true freedom. (American Memory Collection.)

Large plantations could exist only with large numbers of workers to do the hard work of planting, chopping, and picking the cotton. The aftermath of the Civil War threw the South into chaos, with blacks having little training for jobs other than farm work and the plantation system in economic shambles from years of war and neglect. (American Memory Collection.)

A bluesman identified only as Elijah Cox poses for this early-20th-century photograph. The musical traditions of the farms grew as access to instruments such as guitars, fiddles, and mandolins became more common. These instruments were rare and prized possessions of Southern farm families. (American Memory Collection.)

This 1911 photograph shows a bluesman identified simply as "Happy Mose" with a banjo. Although rarely used for blues today, the banjo was a common instrument in the early part of the 20th century when the guitar became more common. The word blues was a description for the "down low" feeling of being wronged, whether in the workplace or in matters of romance. (American Memory Collection.)

Blues sprang for a number of primitive traditional forms of music. The primary basis was the "field holler," the call-and-response style of singing that helped to pass the time in the cotton fields or for work gangs on the levee. Parallel to the development of the blues genre was that of spiritual music, which was similar in every way but the subject matter. Spirituals eschewed the carnal and cleaved strictly to the Bible for its guidance and development. (American Memory Collection.)

From before the Civil War until mechanization brought an end to sharecropping, the cotton field was the great social stage where stories, songs, and gossip made the long days go a little faster. On many plantations, hundreds of people would be in the fields chopping or picking cotton. The work was exceedingly hard, the hours long, the weather unforgiving, and the pay low. (American Memory Collection.)

The Blues was a form of "distraction"

Saturday afternoons and all day on Sunday were times of rest and relaxation on the large plantations. Neighbors who had labored in the fields all week would come together for fish fries and house parties on Saturday night. It was said that the devil owned Saturday night, and the Lord owned Sunday. (American Memory Collection.)

Blues music was scorned from the pulpit as "the Devil's music" by preachers through the South. Spouses and grandparents prayed for the souls of the wayward bluesmen. Somehow the music survived intact. Prison work crews and chain gangs added to the themes of one man calling and the rest of the group responding in unison. With the advent of radio, blues became more common and more palatable to the masses, especially for those who did not live on the farm. (American Memory Collection.)

The Blues was uncommon to city folk and uncencored on many topics.

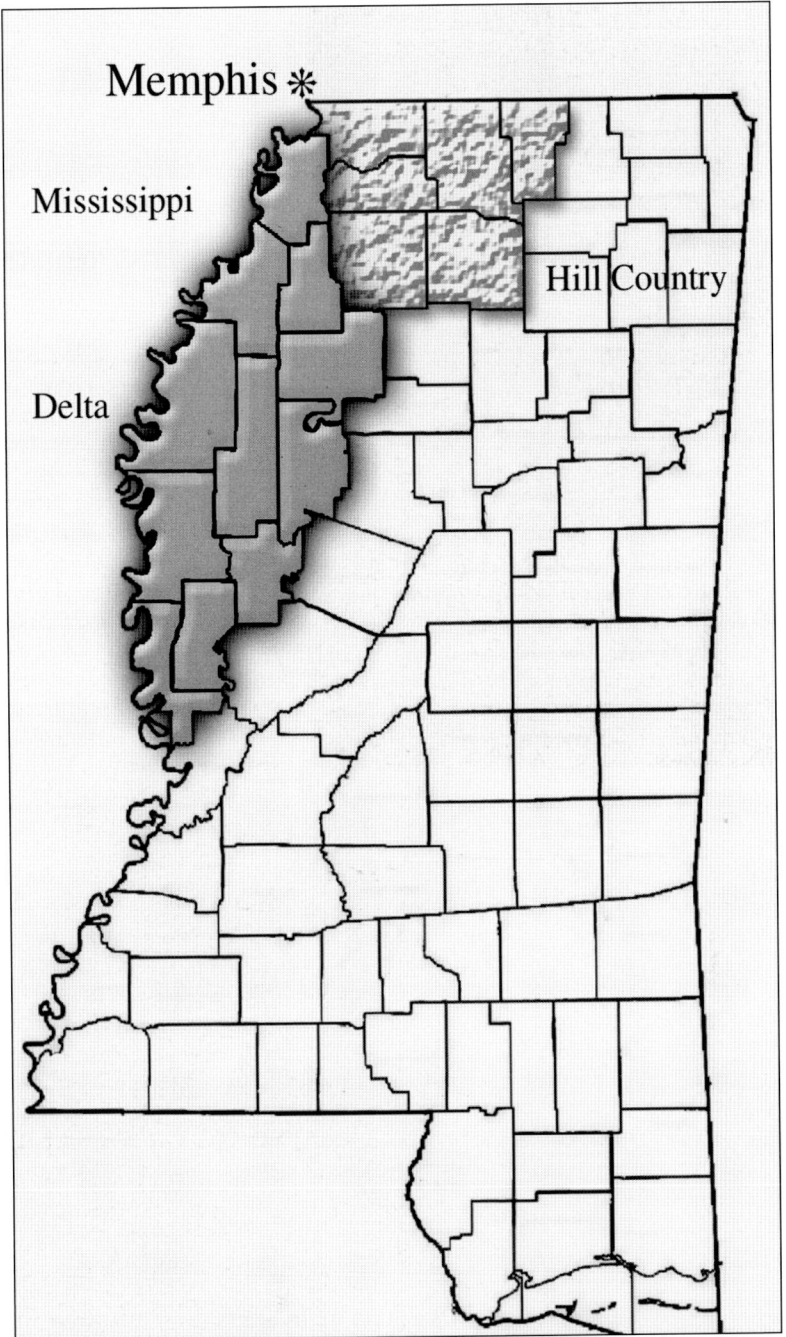

Greenville, Mississippi, author David Cohn wrote that the Delta started in the lobby of the Peabody Hotel in Memphis and ended on Catfish Row in Vicksburg. The Delta is the crescent-shaped body of land that is the Yazoo-Mississippi Delta and not the actual delta of the Mississippi River. The 200-mile-long and 80-mile-wide Delta is truly the birthplace of the blues. The Mississippi Hill Country lacked the large concentrations of African Americans on plantations, but had its population of poor sharecroppers who developed a harder-edged style of blues now called hill country blues. (© W. Bearden.)

Hill country Blues = Hardcore blues. 19

Dockery Plantation, just outside Cleveland and just west of Ruleville, Mississippi, was home to some of the legends of Delta blues. At one time or another, Charley Patton, Howlin' Wolf, Pop Staples, Bukka White, and countless other bluesmen worked or visited on Dockery. Begun by Joe Rice Dockery and later run by his son, Will, the plantation is said to have been one of the best run and most honest operations in the Delta. (© W. Bearden.)

Fred McDowell looks on as Napolean Strickland plays a "diddlybow," a rudimentary instrument developed in the Delta and credited by many bluesmen as their first musical instrument. The diddlybow is made by stretching a length of baling or fence wire between two nails that have been hammered into the outside wall of the house or on a porch post. The wire is made taut by shoving a glass bottle tightly toward each nail. The string is then strummed while another bottle is moved along its length to create notes and a moaning slide effect. With the house acting as a giant resonator, the sound fills the air. Necessity is the mother of the blues. (© Dr. David Evans.)

The Mississippi Delta is one of the few places left in the United States that has held onto its regional identity to a great degree. In many ways, the old traditions are still alive. The proprietor of the Bill Booser Chicken Shack in Leland, Mississippi, Bill Jones, lived his entire life in Washington County and knew King of the Delta Blues Robert Johnson. (Photograph by Steve Roberts, © 1998.)

A young William Christopher Handy is shown here in his band uniform as a cornet player in a minstrel show. Born in Florence, Alabama, Handy was a young orchestra leader in 1903 when he heard what was to become known as the blues for the first time. Handy was waiting for a late-night train in Tutwiler, Mississippi, when he heard a man playing a guitar using a pocketknife for a slide and singing the words, "going to where the Southern 'cross the Dog." This man's late-night lament was to resonate with Handy, who took the form and wrote it down, which became his first blues composition, a campaign tune entitled "Mr. Crump," which was later rewritten and called "Memphis Blues." (American Memory Collection.)

the Blues was solely written from the soul, not the rules.

The "Beale Street Blues" was one of the first and most popular of Handy's compositions. Because of the difficulties of finding a suitable publishing deal, Handy began to publish his own work and achieved a great degree of success. He moved the company to New York City in 1917, where it remains today. (American Memory Collection.)

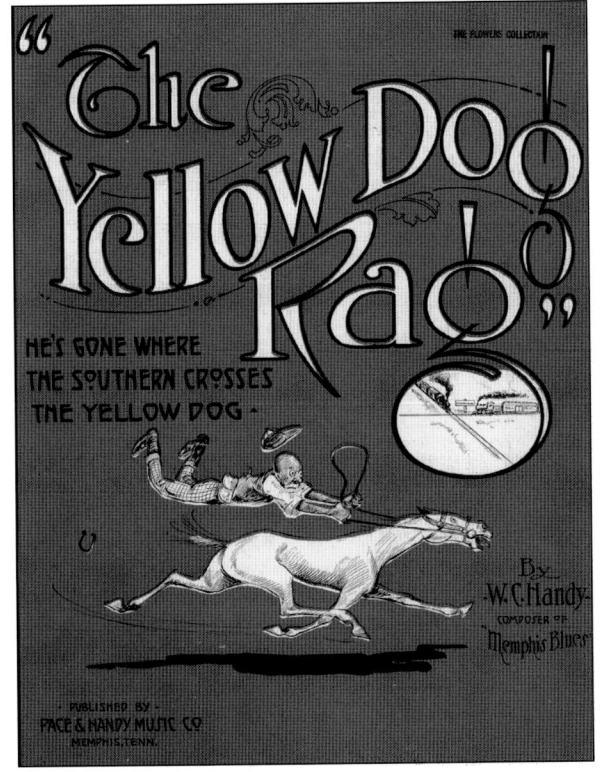

The "Yellow Dog Rag" was written as a reference to the original blues line that Handy heard in 1903. Known locally as the "Yellow Dog," the Yazoo and Mississippi Valley Railroad intersected with the Southern Railroad in Moorhead, Mississippi. (American Memory Collection.)

In 1912, Handy went into business with Harry Pace, and they formed the Pace and Handy Publishing Company. The company was immediately successful, but Pace left the partnership in 1920 to pursue the record business, creating Black Swan Records, an early minority-owned company catering to African American artists. (American Memory Collection.)

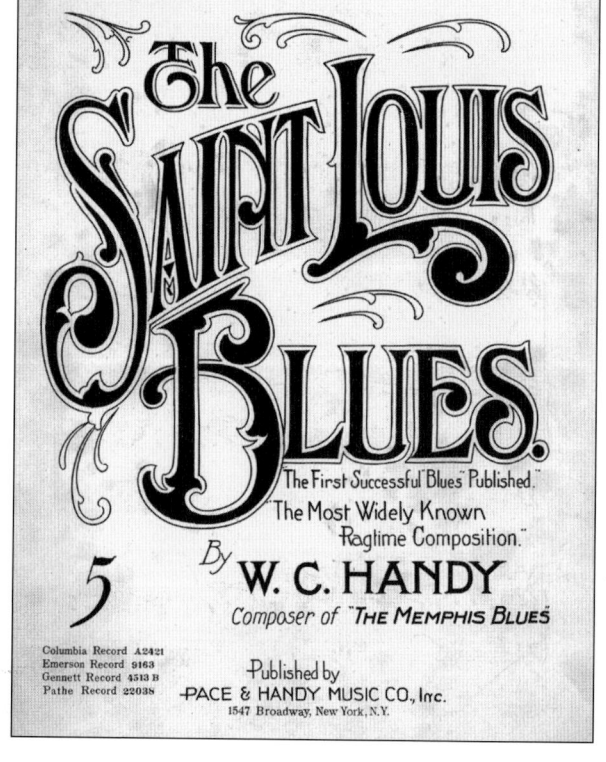

Blues singer Bessie Smith recorded Handy's composition "The St. Louis Blues" in 1925. Smith later starred in a motion picture of the same name. Handy worked with director Kenneth Adams on the film. The blues was spreading beyond the South to an adoring America. (American Memory Collection.)

The style of blues played by Handy and his contemporaries was a very different music than we know as blues today. It was more akin to ragtime with a jaunty beat. The bands were more like orchestras, with banjoes, trumpets, saxophones, and clarinets. It was to be several years before an authentic Delta style was to be heard in the blues. This early Beale Street band had many classically trained members who had probably never worked on a cotton plantation. (© 2005 Center for Southern Folklore Archives.)

At the end of the Civil War, a new economic model was needed. Plantation owners had land but little money for labor, and African Americans had little access to money for the purchase of farmland. A system of sharecropping was developed whereby tenant farmers worked for a year with the landowner taking care of their living expenses and then "settled up" after the cotton crop was harvested and sold. The system was deeply flawed but remained intact until the 1960s. (American Memory Collection.)

MISSISSIPPI JOHN HURT
—1928 SESSIONS—

1065

BURGER

"Mississippi" John Smith Hurt was born in Avalon, Mississippi, in 1892. He first recorded for the Okeh Record label in the late 1920s. The Great Depression put an end to what had been a robust "race records" business, and Hurt lived in obscurity until the early 1960s when he was "rediscovered" by a musicologist named Thomas Hoskins. Hurt's fortunes changed, and he spent the last years of his life playing folk and blues festivals, appearing on television, and recording many albums for Vanguard and Piedmont Records. John Hurt died on November 2, 1966, in Grenada, Mississippi. (Memphis Room Archive.)

By the time he died on August 16, 1938, Robert Johnson had recorded only 42 tracks. That legacy has continued to grow, most likely due to the legends and controversy that surround the "King of the Delta Blues." Johnson was said to have made a deal with the Devil: in exchange for the ability to play the guitar better than anyone else in the Delta, Johnson would sell his soul. Johnson's high-pitched voice is haunting indeed, and his guitar prowess is undeniable, but the facts surrounding his death support a much more ordinary demise. Johnson was a known ladies' man and gambler and evidently crossed the wrong man. Johnson was poisoned and died in Greenwood, Mississippi. (Photograph by Lamar Sorrento.)

Deal w/ Devil

Robert Johnson was surely influenced by Son House and Charley Patton, two lions of the Delta. Johnson's unique style of fingerpicking and the raw emotion of his voice have caused many to call him the greatest blues singer of all time. Say what you will, but Robert Johnson has been much more successful in death than he ever was in life. His legend has spawned the release of countless record compilations, and thousands of covers of his compositions, from Eric Clapton and Keith Richards to virtually every fledgling blues band in the world. There have been books written and films produced about Robert Johnson, and his legend only seems to grow with time. (Photograph by Lamar Sorrento.)

29

The juke joint was an outgrowth of house parties and backroom gambling in the shotgun shacks of the rural areas and small towns of the Delta. An enterprising businessman would open a "café" and offer food, bootleg whiskey, beer, and a place to dance and shoot craps. These juke joints were the training ground for countless bluesmen. It was a place to work out songs because no band ever played a song for only three minutes—that was the limitation of a record—but in the joints, a song could and would last for 15 or 20 minutes, creating a groove deep enough to feel in your bones. Although many have been closed down over the years, the juke joint is still a tradition in the Delta. (American Memory Collection.)

Two

BLUES FINDS A HOME

By the 1920s, Beale Street had become the Main Street for African Americans living in Memphis. A. Schwab opened at 163 Beale in 1876 as a dry goods store, supplying household goods and clothing for neighborhood residents, and is still in business more than 130 years later. Their motto is, "If we don't have it, you don't need it." (Memphis Room Archive.)

A jug band entertains on Beale Street in 1949. These bands played vaudeville, blues, and country music with mostly homemade musical instruments such as a washtub bass, a whiskey jug, banjoes and mandolins made from gourds or cigar boxes, and a washboard. The best known Memphis jug band was Gus Cannon's Jug Stompers, who regularly played Beale Street and scored a hit with the much-covered "Walk Right In." (Memphis Room Archive.)

Memphis was a divided city until the mid-1960s, with separate facilities for whites and blacks. Beale Street was somewhat exempt from these segregation laws in that whites frequented the blues clubs on a regular basis. Signs such as the one pictured were seen in Memphis until the 1970s. (© Steve Roberts.)

Beale Street was a bustling area with streetcars and crowded sidewalks until the urban renewal fiasco of the late 1960s, which caused whole neighborhoods to be torn down in the hopes that it would cure the widespread poverty in the area. With the people gone, shops, restaurants, and nightclubs had little choice but to close their doors, thus creating more urban blight. (Memphis Room Archive.)

Robert Henry's shoe shop on Beale Street was a center of activity on a number of fronts. It was a gathering place for locals, a place to have your shoes half-soled, and also an agency for booking bands on Beale Street. Musicians regularly stopped by for gossip and the chance to find a gig. (© 2005 Center for Southern Folklore Archives.)

Club Handy was an institution on Beale Street for many years. Anyone playing blues from the 1940s through the 1960s played Club Handy. B. B. King played his first gigs with the Bill Harvey Band at Club Handy. (Memphis Room Archive.)

In his musical composition "Beale Street Blues," Handy wrote, "If Beale Street could talk, if Beale Street could talk, married men would have to take their beds and walk, except one or two who never drink booze, and the blind man on the corner singing the 'Beale Street Blues.' " (Memphis Room Archive.)

WDIA was the first radio station in America to be programmed solely by African Americans. Known as the Goodwill Station, WDIA quickly became the place where Memphis blacks got their news and entertainment. Disk jockeys Nat D. Williams, Rufus Thomas, and A. C. Williams quickly became stars in their own right. A young B. B. King made his radio debut on WDIA in 1949 and wrote and performed his first jingle touting the curative powers of "Pepticon." (Memphis Room Archive.)

Nat D. Williams was the first African American to host a show on WDIA. At that time, Memphis's population was over 40 percent African American, yet no radio station addressed them. When Williams's "Tan Town Jamboree" premiered on October 25, 1948, the response was tremendous, except for the bomb threats called in by the white segregationists. WDIA began playing blues records, and the rest is history. The station continues to lead in the ratings even today, an unheard-of feat owing to the fact that WDIA is an AM station. (© 2005 Center for Southern Folklore Archives.)

A collection of nightclub tickets and raffle tickets from 1960s-era Beale Street is shown here. Andrew "Sunbeam" Mitchell owned the Club Handy; the Mitchell Hotel, where touring blues musicians stayed; and the Mitchell Grill. (Memphis Room Archive, Beale Street Development Corporation Collection.)

Chester "Howlin' Wolf" Burnett was one of the all-time unique performers to come on the Memphis music scene. Sam Phillips recorded some of the greatest blues songs in history with Wolf in the early 1950s. Howlin' Wolf grew up in West Point, Mississippi, and began playing guitar at age 18 when he met Charley Patton. His family later moved to Parkin, Arkansas, where Chester began playing the area juke joints. He stood over 6-feet 4-inches tall and weighed around 300 pounds. His career kicked into high gear when he opened shows in England for the Rolling Stones and other blues-based "British Invasion" acts. Suffering from kidney trouble in his later years, Howlin' Wolf died in 1976 in Chicago. (Memphis Room Archive.)

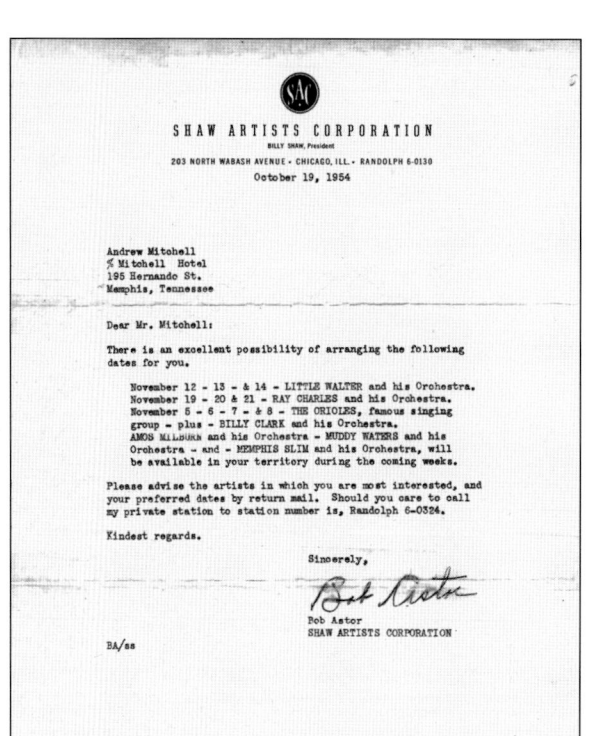

This 1954 letter from The Shaw Artists Corporation representative Bob Astor to Sunbeam Mitchell illustrates the caliber of artists traveling to Beale Street in the 1950s. Little Walter, Ray Charles, Memphis Slim, and Muddy Waters were in their prime as entertainers, and Memphis supported them. It was possible to see world-class blues acts at the Club Handy every week. (Memphis Room Archive.)

The Bill Harvey Band featuring B. B. King agreed to play at Club Handy on January 29, 1955, for the sum of $400. If only we had a film of that performance. (Memphis Room Archive.)

If a picture is worth 1,000 words, this one has to be worth 10,000. Roscoe Gordon, with a rooster perched on his shoulder, is pictured with Sun Records founder Sam Phillips in a promotional shot for Gordon's release of—what else—*The Chicken*. The rooster was named Butch and had several costumes that matched his owner's. The photograph was taken inside Sun Studios at 706 Union Avenue, a shrine of American blues and rock and roll. (Courtesy Knox Phillips.)

With Bobby "Blue" Bland and Little Junior Parker on one bill and a floor show, Sam Rozelle and "Little Jimmy Reed" Douglas, plus the Princess of Shake Dancers on the other, Memphis was in for a treat at these shows. Live entertainment was at its height during the 1950s on Beale Street. It was not to last. (Memphis Room Archive.)

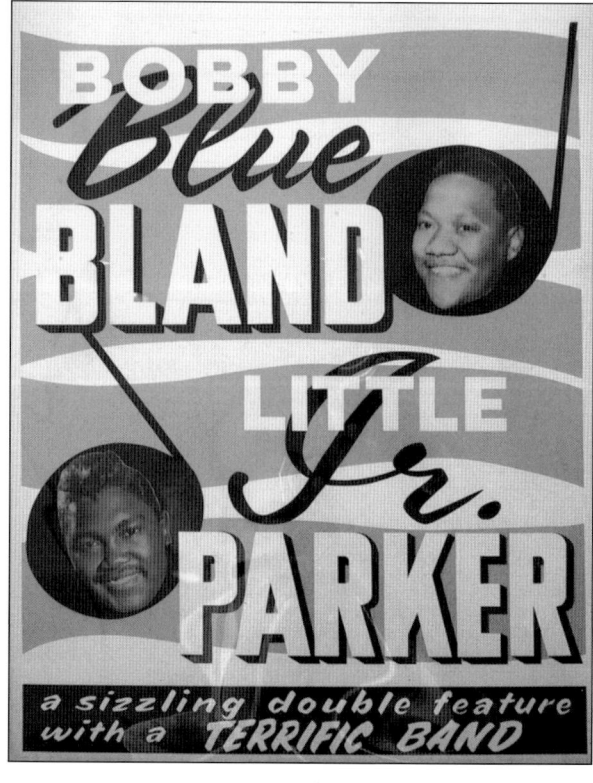

Although always a spot for drinking and gambling, by the 1950s, Beale Street began to see pawn shops occupy former saloons, cafés, and nightclubs. It was a sign of things to come. Beale Street was headed for hard times. (Memphis Room Archive.)

W. C. Handy is shown here on one of his final trips to Memphis, the city where it all came together for him as a young musician. Handy had a keen sense of civic responsibility and rarely turned down the many offers to participate in public events. (Memphis Room Archive.)

Little Willie John's is a classic blues story. From the mid-1950s to the early 1960s, he had a dozen songs on the rhythm and blues charts, making him a Memphis favorite. His song "Fever" was covered by Peggy Lee and made it to the top-10. Known for his hot temper and also known to carry a pistol at all times, Little Willie stabbed and killed a man in Seattle in 1966 and spent the next two years in the Washington State Prison, where he died in 1968. He was 31 years old. (Memphis Room Archive.)

Born in rolling Fork, Mississippi, in 1915, McKinley Morganfield moved at the age of three to Clarksdale, Mississippi, with his grandmother, where they lived on Stovall Plantation. A farm worker for most of his adolescence and young adulthood, Muddy Waters, as he was known, was "discovered" by Alan Lomax in 1941. Lomax was working on a blues project for the Library of Congress and recorded Morganfield in his cabin on the plantation. By 1943, Morganfield had moved to Chicago and soon signed with Chess Records. His sound changed the face of the blues when he began to play an electric guitar. His hard-edged sound was defined further by his attitudes toward authority, money, and women. If any one person personifies the Delta blues, it is Muddy Waters. He died in 1983. (Photographs by Don Bronstein/Chess Records.)

W. C. Handy traveled to Memphis often during the later years of his life and never failed to draw a crowd. Although he had lived in New York City for many years, he thought of Memphis as home. A fall and injury in the New York subway in 1943 left him blind. After his wife's death, he remarried in 1954 to his longtime secretary, Louise Logan. Handy said that she had become his eyes. (Memphis Room Archive.)

The City of Memphis dedicated a park in W. C. Handy's honor in 1931. Even today, blues musicians from around the world can be seen playing at the foot of his statue. Handy wrote a total of five books: *Blues: An Anthology: Complete Words and Music of 53 Great Songs; Book of Negro Spirituals; Father of the Blues: An Autobiography; Unsung Americans Sung;* and *Negro Authors and Composers of the United States.* (Memphis Room Archive.)

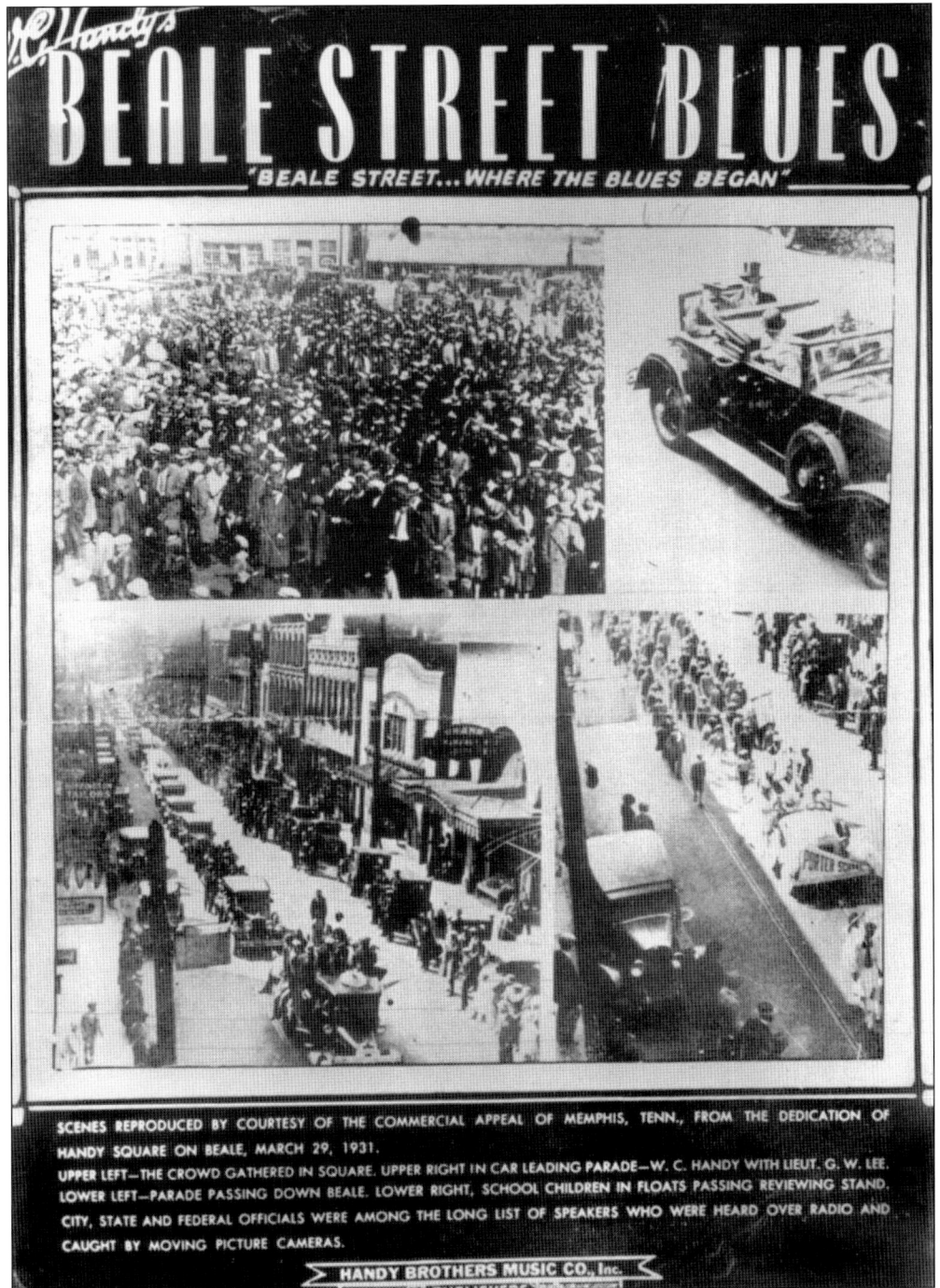

This is a composite of photographs from Handy Brothers Music, printed as a special section by the Memphis Commercial Appeal. Shown are scenes from the dedication of Handy Park on March 29, 1931. Lt. George W. Lee, the first African American to hold an officer's rank in the United States military, is shown riding with Handy in the limousine. (Memphis Room Archive.)

W. C. Handy sat in with a group of Beale Street musicians for this photograph opportunity in 1954. Handy is known as "the Father of the Blues" for being one of the few people in history to introduce a new style of music to the world. He always acknowledged that he did not invent the blues but simply wrote them down and presented them to a worldwide audience. (Memphis Room Archive.)

The Club Handy was a force on Beale Street for many years. It was the site of countless world-class performances and the place that blues musicians called home. (Memphis Room Archive.)

The Handy Theatre was built on Park Avenue in the Orange Mound neighborhood in Memphis and was the home to the popular Wednesday night talent show. The grand prize was $5. (Memphis Room Archive.)

CLUB HANDY

195 Hernando

MON. NITE, FEB. 23 9 'TIL

ADVANCE $1.10   AT DOOR $1.50

. BIG 3 STAR ATTRACTION .

═IN PERSON═

LARRY BIRDSONG

Latest Hit Recording . . .
"EVERY NITE IN THE WEEK"

ROSCO GORDON

"Torro"   "Sally Jo"   "The Chicken"

FLOYD DIXON

Hit Recording . . . "TELEPHONE BLUES"

If there is one person in the pantheon of Memphis music who blurred the lines between blues, rhythm and blues, and rock and roll, it was Dewey Phillips. His *Red, Hot & Blue* radio show on WHBQ AM was the unifying force for blacks and young whites in 1950s and 1960s Memphis. He is best known for being the first DJ to play Elvis's first release, but in reality he is that and much more; he is the true father of rock and roll. Long before Dick Clark was hosting American Bandstand, Dewey was spinning records for dancing teens in Memphis. (University of Memphis Special Collections.)

By the late 1960s, the crowds were beginning to thin on Beale Street, and blues was supplanted by Motown rhythm and blues and rock music. The Club Handy will always be remembered as a place with a warm welcome, hot music, and great atmosphere. (Memphis Room Archive.)

50

Galaxy Artist Management, Inc.
1448 S. Michigan Avenue
Chicago, Illinois 60605

LITTLE MILTON

Chess Recording Artist
2120 S. Michian Avenue
Chicago, Illinois 60616

Little Milton Campbell was born in Inverness, Mississippi, in 1934. He found his passion at an early age and mixed blues, gospel, and country music into a sound all his own. Ike Turner brought Milton to the attention of Memphis producer Sam Phillips in the early 1950s. Milton then moved on to Chicago's Chess Records, where he produced a string of hits like "We're Gonna Make It" and "Grits Ain't Groceries." He was a favorite on the chitlin' circuit of juke joints and later recorded for Stax and Malaco Records. Little Milton died in 2005. (University of Memphis Special Collections.)

Phineas Newborn Jr. was an anomaly in Memphis music. He studied under his father, Phineas Sr., in a rhythm and blues band. He then moved to New York and then California, where he became a respected jazz pianist, recording albums for the Contemporary label. A series of emotional and physical problems plagued Newborn for most of his life, and after a brief comeback, he died in Memphis in 1989. (University of Memphis Special Collections.)

Beale Street was a place where a man could find a drink, a woman, gambling, some music, and a fight, if he weren't careful. Tales abound of confidence men and hustlers. Beale was the natural progression of a boomtown populated with people on the make. (Memphis Room Archive.)

This is an early compilation blues album with songs by Bobby "Blue" Bland, Junior Parker, Howlin' Wolf, and Sonny Blair. The record business was in its infancy during the 1950s, and artists jumped labels constantly, recording for anyone with a few dollars and the wherewithal to release a record. (Memphis Room Archive.)

In an effort to appeal to the young white kids who were just getting interested in the blues, Checker Records compiled songs from Muddy Waters, Howlin' Wolf, and Bo Diddley. They could see that a change was coming, and they wanted to cash in on this new audience. (Memphis Room Archive.)

Beale Street was declared a National Historic District in 1966. The street would see hard times for the next 15 years, when there was virtually no music to be seen or heard anywhere near Beale Street. The world, it seemed, had turned its back on the blues. (Memphis Room Archive.)

Three

KEEPING THE
BLUES ALIVE

Beale Street lay in economic and social ruin by the 1970s. The once-vibrant street was little more than a cruel yet constant reminder of its glory days. The blues was nowhere to be found. (Memphis Room Archive.)

Although roundly debated by some, the "rediscovery" of the blues is credited to a couple of outsiders and some enterprising Memphis young people like Charlie Brown and John McIntyre. Bill Barth (pictured here) and John Fahey came to the South in search of the blues, and they found it in abundance. Finding 1930s bluesman Skip James in a Tunica, Mississippi, hospital, they paid his bill and then took him to the Newport Jazz Festival in 1964, where he began the resurrection of his once-proud career. Barth moved to Memphis in the mid-1960s and helped found the Memphis Country Blues Society, a group that produced several blues festivals and, most important, brought forgotten blues artists to the public's attention. Barth died in Amsterdam, Holland, in 2000. (University of Memphis Special Collections.)

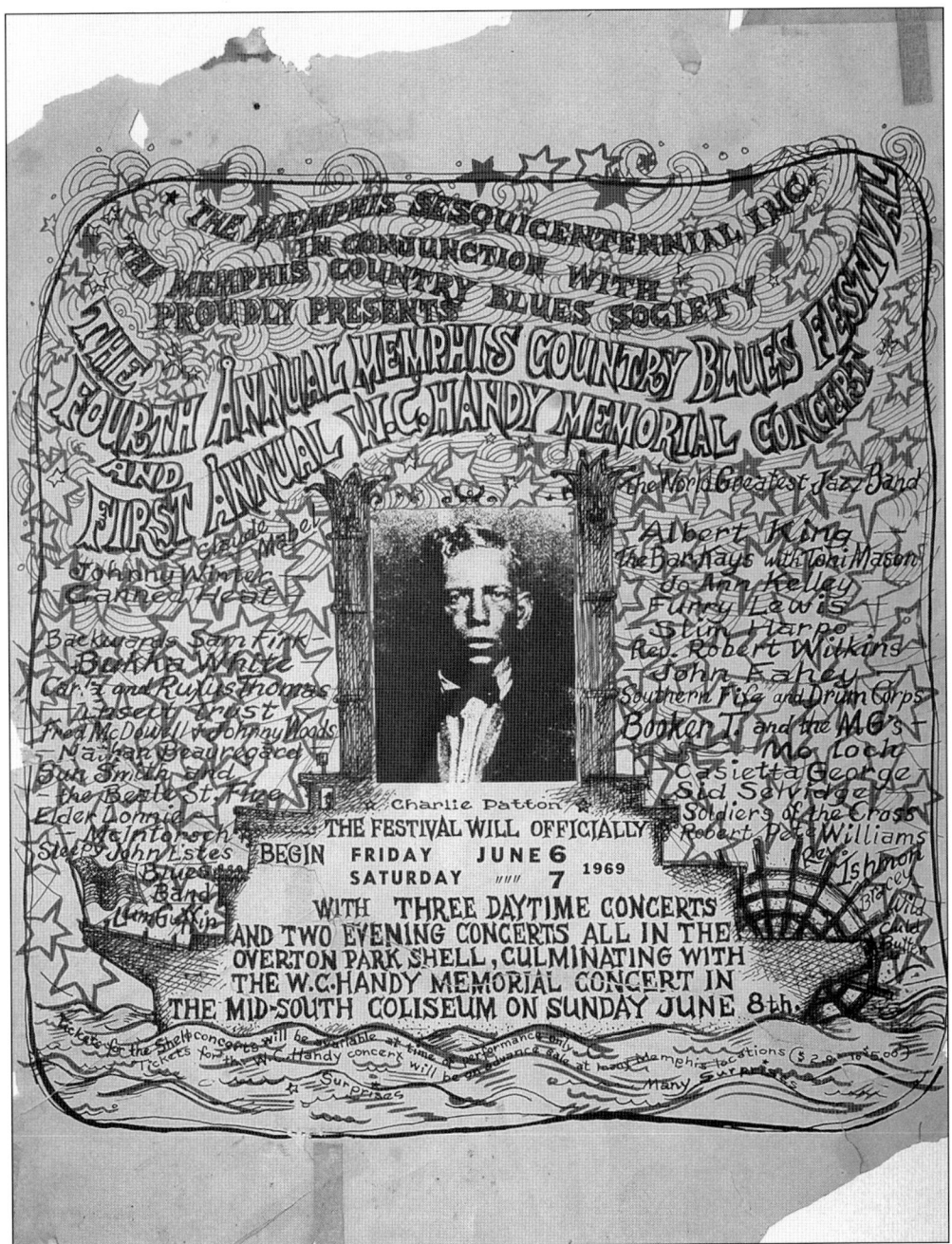

A ragged and worn poster from the fourth Country Blues Festival with the icon of the Delta blues is shown here with Charley Patton looking on with pride. The line-up was a blues lover's dream: Bukka White, Fred McDowell and Johnny Woods, Furry Lewis, Sleepy John Estes, Albert King, Rev. Robert Wilkins, Booker T the MG's, and on and on. The occasion was also the first W. C. Handy Memorial Concert, an event that helped lead to the establishment of the Blues Foundation and the W. C. Handy Awards. (© 2005 Center for Southern Folklore Archives.)

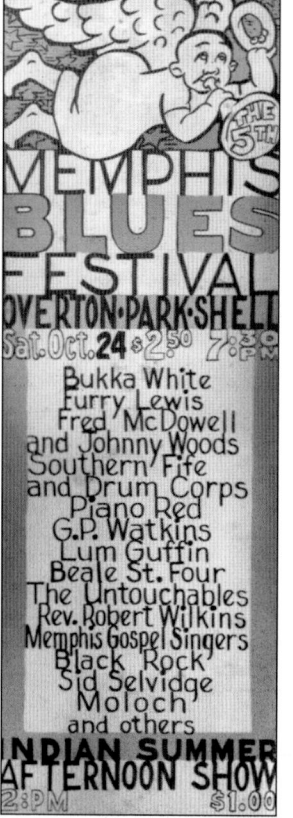

This photograph shows the neo-blues band Moloch performing for the cameras at the June 1969 Country Blues Festival. Playing from left to right are Mike Riddick, Eugene Wilkins, Phillip Durham, Lee Baker, and Fred Nicholson. Memphis blues was again on the rise—this time without rules and with a heavily rock-tinged blues amalgam that shook the foundations of the Overton Park Shell both figuratively and literally. For the entire story, see Robert Gordon's essential book, *It Came From Memphis.* (University of Memphis Special Collections.)

The poster for the fifth annual blues festival is a great piece of 1960s art. The line-up was a blues lover's dream. The place was the Overton Park Shell, which earlier saw Elvis Presley's first public performance, and the price was right. (Save Our Shell.)

MoLoch

Moloch was the incarnation of the Memphis schizophrenic mix of musical styles and genres. The 1969, Don Nix-produced record album *Moloch* included the Nix-penned "Going Down" and "Same Old Blues" and captured the essence of one of Memphis's most unique bands. The sight of Moloch being escorted into Crump Stadium in 1971 by the Memphis motorcycle gang "The Family" is a vision not easily forgotten. It was quite simply the defining image of Memphis music in the early 1970s. (University of Memphis Special Collections.)

Nathan Beauregard, blind since his birth in 1863, entertained a packed house at the Overton Park Shell in 1969. Beauregard was led around by his nephew, who was in his 70s. Beauregard was 108 years old at the time and was said by those in attendance to sing with the high-pitched, forlorn wail of a much earlier time. He sang "Nathan's Bumble Bee Blues" and "Bout a Spoonful." (© Sid Selvidge.)

Nathan Beauregard (right) and Rev. Robert Wilkins are shown backstage at the Memphis Country Blues Festival in June 1969. Wilkins swore off the blues and joined the Church of God in Christ, becoming a minister in the mid-1930s, due to the violence he experienced in the Mississippi juke joints. For the rest of his career, he sang gospel songs. (© Dr. Douglas Cupples.)

DON NIX

shelter
recording
company

In classic Memphis fashion and with a biography almost too good to be true, Don Nix was a founding member of the Mar-Keys with Packy Axton, Steve Cropper, Duck Dunn, Wayne Jackson, Terry Dunn, and Smoochie Smith. They scored a hit with "Last Night" in 1961. In the mid-1960s, Nix struck up a friendship with Tulsa songwriter and producer Leon Russell and began touring with Dick Clark's Caravan of Stars, backing Gary Lewis and the Playboys, one of Russell's acts. Nix quickly learned his way around the recording studio and began producing artists on his own. Nix spent the next several years writing and producing for artists such as Freddie King, Albert King, Jeff Beck, Sid Selvidge, Charlie Musselwhite, and John Mayall, among others. His composition "Goin' Down" has been recorded by J. J. Cale, Luther Allison, Jeff Beck, Moloch, Bruce Chanel, John Lee Hooker, and dozens of others. Don Nix is a musician, producer, photographer, writer, and the chief "keeper of the flame" for Memphis music. (© Don Nix.)

Don Nix and Walter "Furry" Lewis are pictured here in Lewis's bedroom in 1971. Nix and other Memphis musicians became fast friends with Lewis, finding him gigs that paid more in a night than he made in a month. The sign above his bed reads, "Please Lord help me keep my dam nose out of other people business"—good advice from years of experience. (© Don Nix.)

Sid Selvidge and Furry Lewis became friends in the late 1960s and remained close until Lewis's death in 1981. Lewis, who had lost a leg in a railroad accident in 1917 while hoboing around the country, soon came back to Memphis where he performed on Beale Street, primarily as a solo act but frequently with Gus Cannon and Will Shade. He recorded his first record for the Vocalian label in 1927. (© Sid Selvidge.)

In what has to be one of the finest photographs ever taken of a blues artist, Furry Lewis poses showing his empty wallet, his guitar there on the bed beside him, his "box" containing a pint of Hiram Walker Ten High whiskey, a couple of packs of Pall Mall cigarettes, and his pistol laying close at hand. During the "Blues Revival" of the late 1960s, Lewis was a favorite with young audiences who appreciated his charm, jokes, and mastery of the guitar. He turned his newfound celebrity into a guest appearance on *The Tonight Show with Johnny Carson*, a role in the Burt Reynold's movie *W. W. and the Dixie Dance Kings*, and large concert venues as part of Don Nix's Alabama State Troupers. When asked by Johnny Carson if he was married, he replied, in classic Lewis fashion, "Why do I need a wife when the man next door's got one?" (University of Memphis Special Collections.)

Furry Lewis and friend Clara Thomas pose in this 1976 photograph. *The Memphis Press Scimitar* ran a story on Furry and one of the many rebirths of Memphis blues. Furry held court in his bedroom, often sitting on the bed with his prosthetic leg removed. Joni Mitchell sang of the scene in her 1975 "Furry Sings the Blues," which appeared on the album *Hejira*. (University of Memphis Special Collections.)

To say that Jim Dickinson is a legend is a gross understatement. He is the godfather, the grand poobah, the arbiter of taste, and various other titles that would have to be made up. His accomplishments are vast but some favorites are that he was a friend and confidant to Furry Lewis, played on the Rolling Stones' recording of "Wild Horses," produced the album *Beale Street Saturday Night*, contributed to the film soundtrack *The Long Riders*, and performed with Mudboy and the Neutrons. To further appreciate Jim Dickinson, you really must read Robert Gordon's *It Came From Memphis*. (© 1979 Center for Southern Folklore Archives; photograph by Robert T. Jones Jr.)

Albert King was born on April 25, 1923, in Indianola, Mississippi. His birth name was Albert Nelson, but he picked up the King from B. B., who was not related, although Albert would sometimes claim that B. B. was his half-brother. The family moved to Osceola, Arkansas, in 1931, and King learned all too well the life of a sharecropper. He was a big man, standing six-foot-four and weighing over 250 pounds. King played his trademark Gibson Flying V left-handed. He recorded for Stax Records for many years, scoring hits such as "Crosscut Saw" and "Born Under a Bad Sign." (Memphis Room Archive.)

ALBERT KING

Bukka White was born sometime in the early 1900s in either Aberdeen or Houston, Mississippi. He grew up farming and had stints as a hobo, a semi-pro baseball player, and a boxer. He had a measure of success in the music business in the late 1930s, actually recording a record while he was a prisoner at the Mississippi State Penitentiary at Parchman. "Rediscovered" in the late 1960s, he revived his recording career and went on to play festivals across the country until his death in 1977. (© Dr. Douglas Cupples.)

Little Laura Dukes learned guitar from Robert Nighthawk in the early 1930s. Her father had been a drummer in W. C. Handy's band. Little Laura worked Memphis clubs and parties as a dancer and singer with Will Batts South Memphis Jug Band and traveled throughout the South with Charlie Banks and his Beale Street Originals. She was a fixture at the old Blues Alley club on Front Street in Memphis during the 1970s. (© 2005 Center for Southern Folklore Archives; photograph by Ray Allen.)

Jessie May Hemphill is the granddaughter of North Mississippi Hill Country fife and drum bandleader Sid Hemphill. She was born in Senatobia, Mississippi, on October 13, 1933. Jessie May is a powerful guitarist, songwriter, and vocalist specializing in the North Mississippi country blues traditions of her regional and family heritage. Shown here with University of Memphis ethnomusicologist David Evans, she was first recorded on the university's High Water recording label. Her 1981 "She Wolf" album was released in France on the Vogue label. Jessie May's first full-length American album, *Feelin' Good*, was released in 1990 and won a Handy Award for best acoustic album of the year. In 1993, she suffered a stroke that left her paralyzed on the left side. Unable to play guitar, Hemphill retired from her career. (The Blues Foundation Archive.)

Uncle Ben Perry was a fixture on Beale Street for many years, one of the few true street musicians, playing for quarters and the odd dollar bill. His enduring legacy is that scores of aspiring bluesmen sat in with him in and around Handy Park as his nephews. (© Steve Roberts.)

James "Son" Thomas was an unlikely success story. He lived his entire life in or around Leland, Mississippi, and if it had not been for his "discovery" by William Ferris, he might have lived out his life in obscurity. He was a fine singer, guitarist, and folk artist and was called the "last of the Delta bluesmen." Ferris wrote about Thomas in his 1968 book, *Blues From the Delta*, and featured Thomas in several films produced by the Center for Southern Folklore. Son Thomas worked much of life as a gravedigger. His clay skulls and other art spoke of the darker side of Delta culture. He was a regular performer at the Delta Blues Festival held each September in Greenville, Mississippi. (Top © Rae Nell Hunter; Bottom © Don Nix.)

Bukka White is shown here holding court on the back steps of his house in Memphis. White was approachable but suffered no fools. He was a tough man who had been to jail and seen the hard side of life. That hard edge came across in his music. (© Sid Selvidge.)

Sam Chatmon grew up as a part of a musical family. Delta legend Charley Patton was his half-brother, and he played with other family members in the Mississippi Sheiks. Chatmon moved to Hollandale in the early 1940s and worked on plantations until being "rediscovered" during the 1960s. He played at Delta parties and appeared at blues festivals across the United States. He died in 1983 at the age of 86. (© Mississippi ETV.)

Don Nix was on top of the music world when he put his Alabama State Troupers tour together in 1972. Lonnie Mack was in the original line-up but was replaced by Furry Lewis. Nix introduced thousands of young blues lovers to the delights of Lewis's playing and singing. Nix helped to bring the blues back to life and was an open and generous musician who shared the limelight with everyone who appeared with him. (© Don Nix.)

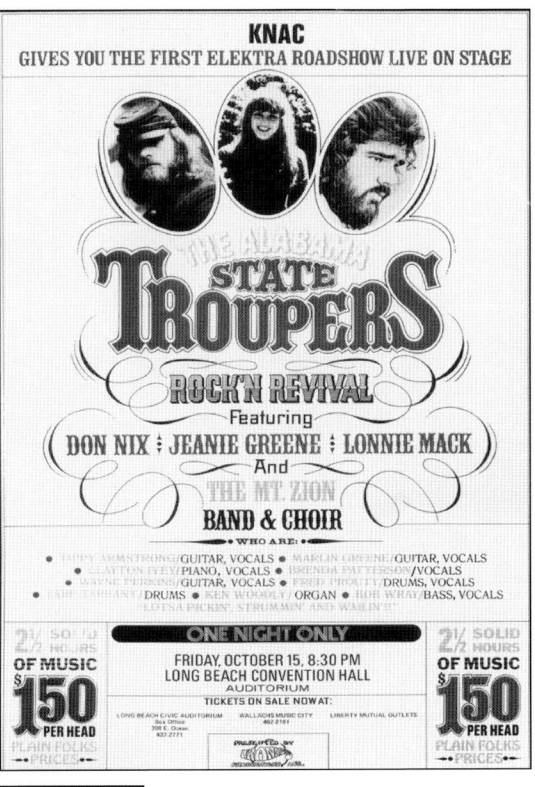

Although known as "Soulsville, USA," Stax Records was a home to many blues greats. Gus Cannon and Albert King were well-known blues artists who had record deals with the label. By the early 1970s, Stax had fallen on hard times, partly due to the deaths of Otis Redding and five members of the Bar Kays and partly due to losing its distribution deal with Atlantic Records. The label filed for bankruptcy in 1976, and the studio was bulldozed in 1981. Today the Stax Museum, which was built on the site of the original studio, attracts thousands of soul and blues fans annually. (University of Memphis Special Collections.)

Roebuck "Pops" Staples is unique in that he successfully created music that was a mix of blues and gospel at a time when the world needed to hear positive messages in its music. Joined by his daughters—Mavis, Pervis, Yvonne, and Cleotha—Pops steered the group through a number of hits in the early 1970s, such as "Respect Yourself" and "I'll Take You There." Born on a farm in Winona, Mississippi, Staples worked his way up the musical ladder by sticking to his high moral standards and commitment to his family. (University of Memphis Special Collections.)

Bobby "Blue" Bland has been one of Memphis's most successful bluesmen and has continued to record and tour since coming on the scene in the early 1950s. His greatest recordings—"Turn On Your Love Light," "Stormy Monday Blues," and "I Pity the Fool"—are required listening for anyone wanting to hear the progression of the blues from the 1950s to the 1970s. He was honored by the Blues Foundation with a Lifetime Achievement Award in 1999 and was inducted into the Rock and Roll Hall of Fame in 1992. (© Steve Roberts.)

Rufus Thomas was a force of nature. From his earliest performances with the Rabbits Foot Minstrels to his last performances before his death in 2001, he was man of firsts. He had the first hit, "Bearcat" on Sam Phillips's Sun label. He had the first hit, "Cause I Love You" with daughter Carla on the Satellite label, which was soon to become Stax Records. He was among the first deejays on the first African American–programmed radio station, WDIA. Thomas was also a tireless ambassador for Memphis music, traveling around the globe spreading his goodtime beat and teaching the world how to "do the Funky Chicken" and "Walk the Dog." He was called "the world's oldest teenager" and for good reason—Thomas could out-dance, out-sing, and out-perform people half his age. His bright handmade costumes with capes, knee-high boots, and short pants were truly a thing of beauty. (© 1989 Center for Southern Folklore Archives; photograph by Robert T. Jones Jr.)

An anonymous street musician was a sign of change coming to Beale Street in the early 1980s. The city had struggled with plans for the area, knowing that an entertainment district was needed to bring tourists and Memphians back downtown. (© Steve Roberts.)

Willie Blackwell quenches his thirst during a 1971 performance. Blues was being recognized as a key to the growth of Memphis. After years of neglect and inattention, suddenly the blues was cool again. (University of Memphis Special Collections.)

Peter Chatmon, also known as "Memphis Slim," is shown here with Phineas Newborn Jr. on piano. Memphis Slim was one of the greatest piano players and composers to come out of the Memphis scene. A highly prolific artist, he recorded for a number of record labels throughout the 1930s, 1940s, and 1950s. In 1962, he moved to Paris, where he felt he received the respect he deserved. His "Mother Earth" is one of the finest down-tempo blues songs ever recorded. Memphis Slim died in Paris in 1988. (© 1985 Center for Southern Folklore Archives; photograph by Judy Peiser.)

In a publicity shot from Stax Records in 1973, the promotional text reads: "Stax's Albert King is shown singing his recent single, 'I'll Sing the Blues for You,' 'Breaking Up Somebody's Home' and 'Little Brother' during the recent taping of the 90-minute television special presented by Merv Griffin and Stax Records which will air in late January. The show was taped in the Circus Maximus at Caesars Palace in Las Vegas, and features King along with host Isaac Hayes, The Staple Singers, The Emotions, Carla Thomas, Luther Ingram and the Isaac Hayes Dancers." (Memphis Room Archives.)

Stax's Albert King is shown singing his recent hit single, "I'll Sing the Blues for You", "Breaking Up Somebody's Home" & "Little Brother" during the recent taping of the 90-minute television special presented by Merv Griffin and Stax Records which will air in late January. The show was taped in the Circus Maximus at Caesar's Palace in Las Vegas and features King along with host Isaac Hayes, The Staple Singers, The Emotions, Carla Thomas, Luther Ingram, Johnnie Taylor and the Isaac Hayes Dancers

In May 2005, Koko Taylor won a W. C. Handy Award for Traditional Female Blues Artist of the Year. It was her 25th Handy Award and placed her in that rarefied position of being the only blues artist to have ever won 25 Handys. She is the undisputed "Queen of the Blues." (© Steve Roberts.)

Not many people had heard of Johnny Woods (left) when he came along with Fred McDowell to the 1969 Memphis Country Blues Festival. The crowd quickly heard what Fred must have known all along—Johnny could play. A recording of their performance is included on Blue Thumb's *Memphis Swamp Jam*. Although Fred had recorded many albums, he still worked at a service station in Como, Mississippi. McDowell's comment—"I do not play no rock and roll, ya'll. I play the straight natural blues."—resonated with his many fans. (© Don Nix.)

Leland, Mississippi–born bluesman Don McMinn exposes himself to the blues in Handy Park on Beale Street in the early 1980s. Beale was struggling to make a comeback, and McMinn was one of the few authentic blues players on the street. He fronted the house band at the Rum Boogie Café for many years. (Rum Boogie Café.)

Looking down the alley toward the New Daisy Theatre, one can almost taste the desperation. Beale Street was making a slow and painful comeback. Initially corporations opened fancy restaurants and clubs that were decidedly not in the character of the blues and Beale Street. Gradually the corporations left, and individuals opened businesses with a more authentic feel of the culture. (Memphis Room Archives.)

Joe Savarin stands in front of the W. C. Handy House, which had been moved to Beale Street from its original location at 659 Jennette Place. This is where Handy lived when he wrote such classics as "Yellow Dog Blues" and "Beale Street Blues." The small shotgun house was home to Handy, his wife, and six children. Joe Savarin was among those Memphians who organized the Blues Foundation and served as its first executive director. (The Blues Foundation Archive.)

Rufus Thomas (left) and Al Green (right) pose here in their 1970s finery. Rufus was one of the most visible celebrities on the Memphis music scene, often emceeing awards shows and benefit events. Al Green grew up singing gospel music and teamed up with Memphis producer Willie Mitchell to chart a string of hits on the Hi Records label through the 1970s. (University of Memphis Special Collections.)

Led by bluesman Will Roy Sanders, the Fieldstones were a Memphis treasure who were virtually unknown outside their neighborhood. Dr. David Evans recorded them on the University of Memphis High Water label and introduced them to the world. (© Dr. David Evans.)

If anyone can be called "The Originator," it has to be Bo Diddley. His hard, insistent rhythms changed the music world and created a bridge from blues to rhythm and blues and rock and roll. Born Ellas McDaniel in McComb, Mississippi, he was inspired to play the guitar after seeing John Lee Hooker perform. (© Steve Roberts.)

That "little ole band from Texas" ZZ Top took a little bit of Texas blues and a huge slice of Memphis blues and soul attitude and became one of the most successful blues bands in the world. The band solidified their signature sound and in 1973 began recording their albums in Memphis. (© Steve Roberts.)

Evelyn Young was one of the only (if not the only) woman to be accepted and respected by the small circle of Memphis musicians. She was a regular at the Club Handy, the Hippodrome, and later Blues Alley. She was featured in the Center for Southern Culture's Robert Gordon–produced *All Day and All Night*, a must-see for any Memphis blues lover. During her long career, Young, a gifted saxophone player, worked with everyone who was anyone in the blues and jazz worlds, including B. B. King. She died in Memphis in 1993. (© 1989 Center for Southern Folklore Archives; photograph by Robert T. Jones Jr.)

Mose Vinson is shown here with little Leah Barns. An authentic practitioner of barrelhouse piano, Vinson worked for Sam Phillips as a clean-up man and a session pianist. His first album was released in 1997. He was a deeply admired performer and regularly held court at the Center for Southern Folklore. (© 1995 Center for Southern Folklore Archives; photograph by Robert Dye.)

Mudboy and the Neutrons, the sometimes band and rare cosmic occurrence on the Memphis music landscape, is the eclectic sum of about 200 years of musical experience unleashed on lucky audiences with a mix of blues, country, rock, and everything else played on instruments ranging from washboards, banjoes, and mandolins, to keyboards and the occasional guitar. Their performances have been few and the records even fewer. "Known Felons in Drag," "Negro Streets at Dawn," and "They Walk Among Us" are must-haves for anyone wishing to understand Memphis music. Pictured here from left to right are Jimmy Crosthwait, Jim Dickinson, Sid Selvidge, and Lee Baker. Baker, who was a founding member of Moloch, friend and sideman to Furry Lewis (who Lewis called "Lee Bailey"), was tragically murdered in 1996. It is doubtful that Mudboy and the Neutrons will ever perform again. (© Steve Roberts.)

Beginning as an original member of the Mar Keys along with Duck Dunn and Don Nix, then as a founding member of Booker T and the MG's, Steve Cropper pretty much wrote the book on the Memphis sound. His guitar playing has been heard on so many iconic songs, many of which he wrote, that it is hard to imagine Memphis music without him. (© Steve Roberts.)

In the blues world, all roads lead to Memphis. This 1978 photograph illustrates that statement beautifully. From left to right are (first row) Ma Rainey and Furry Lewis; (second row) Mick Jagger, Michael Hooks, Percy Brown, Phineas Newborn Jr., Ron Wood, Bill Wyman, Keith Richards, Prince Gabe, and Irvin Salky. In the last minutes before their July 4, 1975, concert in Memphis, the Rolling Stones insisted that Furry Lewis open for them. Producer Knox Phillips had to break away from a family gathering to arrange for a limo to pick up Lewis, who was ready to leave as soon as his performance was finished. (© Alan Ulmer.)

Four

GETTIN' BACK TO BUSINESS

DON McMINN INVITATIONAL BLUES JAM 1987

JIMMY GRIFFIN   STEVE CROPPER   DON   ALBERT KING   JOE MULHERREN   LANNIE McMILLAN

Beale Street reopened in 1982 amid grand schemes and plans for an adult-themed entertainment district. Don McMinn helped to create a sense of legitimacy on the street with blues musicians. The payoff was fun and rewarding. His 1987 blues jam included Jimmy Griffin of Bread fame, Steve Cropper, Albert King, Joe Mulherin, and Lannie McMillan. (Doug McMinn.)

Known primarily for his number-one country music hits "Behind Closed Doors" and "The Most Beautiful Girl," Memphian Charlie Rich (center) was an early Sun Records rockabilly star. Memphis musicians also knew him as a fine jazz and blues pianist. His "Don't Put A Headstone On My Grave" is one of the great Memphis recordings. Pictured here with B. B. King (left) and Rufus Thomas, Rich was yet another Memphis artist to blur the lines between musical genres. (The Blues Foundation Archive.)

Willie Nelson was at the height of his career when he took time out to pursue one of his great loves—the blues. Here he is onstage playing with B. B. King at an early Handy Awards show. (The Blues Foundation Archive.)

B. B. King (left), Bill Ferris (center), and Carl Perkins pose backstage at the Handy Awards. Perkins, who was an accomplished songwriter, shook the world with "Blue Suede Shoes" in the mid-1950s. Elvis Presley's version of the song went to number one. Later songs such as "Matchbox" and "Everybody's Trying to be My Baby" appeared on early Beatles albums. Bill Ferris, who co-founded the Center for Southern Folklore, wrote books and made films about the South and later was the chairman of the National Endowment for the Humanities under Pres. Bill Clinton. (The Blues Foundation Archive.)

Memphis actress Cybill Shepherd entertained the Handy Awards crowd in 1989. Although primarily known for her acting in films like *The Last Picture Show* and the hit television show *Moonlighting*, Shepherd has released nine albums. *Vanilla* was produced by Knox Phillips, and *Talk Memphis To Me* was produced by Sid Selvidge. (The Blues Foundation Archive.)

Internationally known and highly respected photographer Dick Waterman (left) is shown here with Ike Turner at the 2000 Handy Awards. Waterman was a blues pioneer who rediscovered Son House in the early 1960s, managed Bonnie Raitt early in her career, and set the mark for photographers who followed in his footsteps. Waterman was inducted into the Blues Hall of Fame in 2000. His photographs have been collected into several successful books, and his work is regularly presented in galleries across America. (© Bob Sekinger, the Blues Foundation Archive.)

The Blues Brothers, Dan Aykroyd and John Belushi, blew onto the scene in the late 1970s as a skit on *Saturday Night Live*. In 1980, they released a movie by the same name, and the rest is history. Steve Cropper, Duck Dunn, and Willie Hall were among the Memphis musicians who backed the Blues Brothers. The movie introduced an entirely new audience to the joys of Memphis music. The movie has become such a part of the culture that it renders over 10 million hits on a Google search. (© Steve Roberts.)

Stevie Ray Vaughn was at the height of his career when a helicopter crash ended his life in 1990. Vaughn's playing was heavily influenced by Memphis bluesman Albert King, who called himself Stevie's godfather. Vaughn was inducted into the Blues Hall of Fame in 2000. (© Steve Roberts.)

Johnny Winter always knew he was going to play the blues. Growing up in Beaumont, Texas, he and his brother, Edgar, would frequent the black nightclubs, often being the only whites in the place. Johnny Winter was inducted into the Blues Hall of Fame in 1988. (© Steve Roberts.)

Vicksburg, Mississippi, native Willie Dixon, the original "Hoochie Coochie Man" proudly poses with his Handy Award in 1988. During his long career, he worked with and wrote for virtually every Chicago blues artist. He was a Chess Records producer and was one of the most successful and prolific songwriters of his time. He was inducted into the Blues Hall of Fame as a performer in 1980. Dixon died in 1992. (The Blues Foundation Archive.)

Legendary producer Sam Phillips poses here with his Blues Foundation Lifetime Achievement Award. Phillips and Ike Turner (left) worked together throughout the early 1950s, with Turner acting as a talent scout for the fledgling Sun Records. Turner, who was from Clarksdale, Mississippi, had his finger on the pulse of the Delta and brought countless singers, songwriters, and musicians to Memphis to record at Phillips's Memphis Recording Service. It is said that the first rock and roll record was "Rocket 88" sung by Turner's Kings of Rhythm sideman Jackie Brenston and recorded by none other than Sam Phillips. (The Blues Foundation Archive.)

Part of the magic of the annual W. C. Handy Awards show is the synergy between artists. In a match-up never before seen, Taj Mahal (left) performs with octogenarian David "Honeyboy" Edwards. Blues artists tend to be fans as well. (© Steve Roberts.)

In another example of the music world beating a path to Memphis's door, former Lovin' Spoonful front man John Sebastian (left) plays with blues great Yank Rachell in 1996. The Spoonful were admirers of the Memphis Jug Band sound and took their name from a Howlin' Wolf song. Yank Rachell was born in Brownsville, Tennessee, in 1910 and worked extensively with Sleepy John Estes. Rachell, who rode the blues revival of the early 1960s, was one of the few bluesmen to play the mandolin. (The Blues Foundation Archive.)

Along with Don McMinn, Ruby Wilson almost single-handedly brought Beale Street back in the early 1980s. Her commanding stage presence and her incredible vocal range has placed her at the top of the circle of Beale Street performers. In addition to packing them in at B. B. King's club, Ruby travels around the world spreading the good vibe of Memphis blues. (The Blues Foundation Archive.)

Buddy Guy has won over 40 Handy Awards during his long career, including several as Entertainer of the Year. Louisiana born, George "Buddy" Guy was inducted into the Rock and Roll Hall of Fame in a 2005 ceremony by Eric Clapton and B. B. King. Guy is an exciting and mesmerizing performer, often going into the audience with his guitar, playing it behind his back and with his teeth. His early work had a huge effect on British guitarists Clapton, Jeff Beck, and Jimmy Page. Guy owns the popular Chicago nightclub Legends. (© Steve Roberts.)

From left to right, former Blues Foundation executive director Howard Stovall, Rufus Thomas, Bobby Rush, Bob Merliss, and Isaac Hayes are shown here backstage at the Blues Hall of Fame induction ceremony held at the Kennedy Center in Washington, D.C., in 1999. (The Blues Foundation Archive.)

Charlie Musselwhite (left) and Lee Roy Parnell take it home at the 2001 Handy Awards in Memphis. Parnell's blues stylings have earned the artist respect outside his field of country music. With many Handy Awards and Grammy nominations to his credit, Charlie Musselwhite is simply a blues legend. (The Blues Foundation Archive.)

A stage full of giants is pictured here. B. B. King's 70th birthday party turned into a star-studded jam session with, from left to right, (partially hidden) Slash, Jeff Healey, Buddy Guy, Willie Nelson, B. B. King, Sam Moore, and J. Blackfoot onstage at the Orpheum Theatre in Memphis. B. B. King is probably the world's most famous bluesman, with 36 albums to his credit. He celebrated his 80th birthday in 2005 and released *80: B. B. King and Friends*. The B. B. King Museum is scheduled to open in 2006 in Indianola, Mississippi. (© Steve Roberts.)

James Cotton has lived the life of a bluesman. After his parents died, his uncle took him to live with Sonny Boy Williamson in West Helena, Arkansas, who took him under his wing and taught him how to play the harmonica. Cotton went on to play in Muddy Waters's band for many years before starting a band of his own. He has played with everyone from Janis Joplin to Led Zeppelin and the Grateful Dead. James Cotton has been at the top of his game for over 50 years. (© Steve Roberts.)

David Less (second from left) led the Blues Foundation for several years during the early 1990s, establishing many of the awards and performance events that have become the hallmark of the organization. Here he is shown backstage at the Handys with Tracy Nelson and BMI's Roger Sovine (far right). (The Blues Foundation Archive.)

From left to right, Rome McMinn, James Govan, Doug McMinn, Dee Fisk, Don McMinn, and Don Chandler pose on the bandstand of the Rum Boogie Café, one of Beale's most successful nightclubs. Govan and Chandler still play in the house band, now called James Govan and the Boogie Blues Band, and have racked up more performances on Beale Street than any other musicians. (Doug McMinn.)

Keb Mo poses with his Handy Award for his 1999 Blues Song of the Year, "As Soon As I Get Paid." Keb Mo played bluesman Robert Johnson in the highly acclaimed *Can't You Hear the Wind Howl* in 1997. (The Blues Foundation Archive.)

Levon Helm, founding member of the Band, takes the stage at the Handy Awards in 2002. Helm, who grew up in Turkey Scratch, Arkansas, was heavily influenced by Sonny Boy Williamson's performances on KFFA radio's legendary *King Biscuit Time*, as well as Robert Lockwood Jr. and Robert Nighthawk. Levon is a true product of the blues culture in and around Helena, Arkansas. (© Bob Sekinger, the Blues Foundation Archive.)

Robert Lockwood Jr. has the distinction of receiving the first Handy Award for Best Traditional Blues Album in 1980. Lockwood was born in 1915 in Turkey Scratch, Arkansas, and learned to play the guitar from Robert Johnson, who was living with Lockwood's mother. His career has been both long and rewarding. Lockwood began his recording career in 1941, the same year he began playing with Sonny Boy Williamson on the KFFA *King Biscuit Time* blues program. (© David Nester.)

Beale Street guitar ace Preston Shannon and Rufus Thomas play the blues on Beale Street. Shannon's highly touted album, *Midnight in Memphis*, was produced by legendary producer Willie Mitchell. (© Steve Roberts.)

John Mayall has been called the "Godfather of British Blues" and for good reason. He mentored such greats as Mick Fleetwood, John McVie, Eric Clapton, and Jack Bruce. Mayall performed with Etta James, Junior Wells, Buddy Guy, and Albert King in the 1982 comeback film *Blues Alive.* (© Steve Roberts.)

Rufus Thomas and Bonnie Raitt present an award at the 11th annual W. C. Handy Blues Awards. Raitt and Thomas teamed up for an electrifying performance of "Walkin' the Dog" at the 1998 Handy Awards show. It was a magical moment. (The Blues Foundation Archive.)

David "Honeyboy" Edwards traveled the Delta with Robert Johnson in the 1930s. His autobiography, *The World Don't Owe Me Nothin'*, was published in 1998 and is one of the best firsthand accounts of the early days of the blues. He was born in Shaw, Mississippi, in 1915 and now lives in Chicago. Here he is seen performing at the 2004 Handy Awards in Memphis. (© Robin Salant.)

Hubert Sumlin, left, and "Steady Rolling" Bob Margolin take the stage at the 2005 Handy Awards. Longtime Howlin' Wolf sideman and protégé Sumlin plays a raw, straight-ahead Delta style. He was born in Greenwood, Mississippi, in 1931 and raised in Hughes, Arkansas. One of the most respected bluesmen in the world, Bob Margolin was an essential part of the Muddy Waters sound during the 1970s. He has won Handys for Traditional Blues Album of the Year, Blues Band of the Year, and twice for Blues Instrumentalist Guitar Player of the Year. (© Robin Salant.)

This 2002 Handy Awards group photograph says it all—possibly more blues talent than has ever been gathered in one room. The front row reads like the ultimate who's who of the blues: from left to right, Bobby Rush, Ruth Brown, Little Milton, B. B. King, Sam Phillips, Ike Turner, Henry Butler, Odetta, Dr. John, Robert Lockwood Jr., and Rev. Gatemouth Moore. The show had ended with a heartfelt performance by B. B. King in which he talked about his struggles as a young man moving to the city from rural Mississippi and thanked those who helped him along the way. (© David Nester.)

Robert Lockwood Jr., playing his trademark 12-string guitar, entertains the masses at the 2004 Handy Awards show. The Handys moved to the Memphis Convention Center Ballroom after many years at the Orpheum Theatre on Main Street. The sit-down dinner and party-like atmosphere was an instant hit with the crowd. Over 30 acts performed that night, making it the longest Handy show in its 25-year history. (© Robin Salant.)

A great mix of generations and styles is pictured here. Dr. John (left), Kenny Wayne Shepherd (center), and Billy Gibbons pose backstage at the 1997 Handys. Once again in the blues world, all roads lead to Memphis. (The Blues Foundation Archive.)

In one of the most electrifying performances of his career, Bobby Rush, the Hoochie Man, works the crowd to a frenzy in this 2002 Handy Awards performance. Rush has been called the "King of the Chitlin' Circuit," that group of small clubs and juke joints where many performers sharpened their skills. Rush's performances, while sometimes shocking, are uniquely entertaining. He is somewhat of a throwback to an earlier time but as cool as you want it. After having been nominated many times, Bobby Rush won his first Handy for Soul/Blues Male Artist of the Year, a fitting tribute to a talented artist. (© Steve Roberts.)

Rufus Thomas looks sharp for the camera at the 1999 Handy Awards. Rufus hosted the awards with Ruth Brown and performed a memorable "Walkin' the Dog" with Bonnie Raitt. (© David Nester.)

Charlie Musselwhite left Memphis in 1962 to find his fortune in Chicago. He signed with Vanguard Records in 1966 and has continued to record on various labels for almost 40 years. He is known as one of the greatest harmonica players in the world, and his recordings bear this out. He has been a regular at the Handys and has won awards for Blues Band of the Year, Blues Song of the Year, and Blues Album of the Year. (© Robin Salant.)

Mavis Staples and Jon Hornyak are backstage at the 2005 Handys. Staples won awards for Blues Album of the Year, Blues Song of the Year, Soul/Blues Album of the Year, and Soul/Blues Female Artist of the Year. Hornyak is the executive director of the Memphis Chapter of the National Academy of Recording Arts and Sciences. The academy has been at the forefront of honoring those who make the music. They also took a major role in helping New Orleans musicians after Hurricane Katrina through its MusiCares program. (© Robin Salant.)

The Blues Lifetime Achievement Awards have honored such luminaries as B. B. King, Ahmet Ertegun, Bobby Bland, Pinetop Perkins, and Ray Charles, among others. Pictured here at the 1997 awards are, from left to right, (first row) Sam Lay, John Lee Hooker, B. B. King, and Koko Taylor; (second row) Ruby Wilson, Kenny Wayne Shepherd, Keb Mo, Bonnie Raitt, Ruth Brown, Dr. John, Billy Gibbons, and Charlie Musselwhite. (The Blues Foundation Archive.)

Blues divas Maria Muldaur (left) and Traci Nelson perform at the 2001 Handy Awards. Memphis blues great Reba Russell performed as a part of the divas, delivering a rousing set of blues standards. The Handy Awards have provided the special platform for various artists to perform together. (© Bob Sekinger.)

Jay Sieleman stands in front of the wall of signed guitars at the Blues Foundation offices on Union Avenue in Memphis. The foundation has been at the forefront of the blues music world since 1980. Sieleman is the fifth executive director of the organization, which has included Joe Savarin, David Simmons, David Less, and Howard Stovall. With more than 135 affiliated blues organizations in 20 countries around the world, the foundation acts as a focal point for the preservation and promotion of the blues. Its 25-member board is made up of leaders from the corporate, music, and education worlds. In 2005, the organization announced a change of the Handy Awards name to the Blues Music Awards as a move to bring broader attention to the awards and surrounding events. (© W. Bearden.)

Five

THE BLUES TODAY

James and Harold Bonner of the Daddy Mack Blues Band get ready for a recording session at Memphis's Inside Sounds studios. Inside Sounds Records is a vibrant record label that, in its 15-year history, has energized the blues world with authentic Memphis music. The blues is very much alive in the clubs and recording studios of Memphis. (© W. Bearden.)

Longtime blues promoter Jay Sheffield is pictured here with Johnny Jones (left) and Little Milton (right). A Helena, Arkansas, native, Sheffield has represented and booked blues acts in Memphis for over 30 years. Sheffield has been an energetic advocate for Memphis music, serving on the board of governors for the Recording Academy and as a member of the Memphis and Shelby County Music Commission. (© Steve Roberts.)

Mississippi-native Morris Cummings has become a fixture on the Memphis blues scene. Blind since age four, Morris is the very embodiment of the Delta bluesman. Cummings comes from a talented lineage. His cousins, Robert and Mary Diggs, led the famed Memphis Sheiks, and his aunt Mary Tanner played with the "Harps of Melody." Cummings is also a cousin of the late great Willie Dixon. He has been called "a new disciple of the Delta" and the "Real Deal on Beale" by the blues press, and he was rated one of the 10 best harmonica players in the world by *Bluzharp Magazine.* (© Steve Roberts.)

From left to right, Big George Brock, Paul Oscher, Charlie Musselwhite, and Billy Gibson gather around the headstone of harmonica-great Aleck "Sonny Boy Williamson" Miller on August 13, 2005. The gravesite near Tutwiler, Mississippi (the town where W. C. Handy first heard the blues), is a much-visited location in the Delta. The event was organized by Robert Jr. Whithall, editor-in-chief of *Big City Rhythm & Blues Magazine*, and was featured in the magazine's October 2005 issue. (© Keith Soltys, Inside Sounds Records.)

Ike Turner shows off his Handy Award for Best Comeback Album of the Year in this 2000 photograph. Turner played a pivotal role in the development of Memphis music, acting as a talent scout for Sam Phillips and fronting bands around the Mississippi Delta. Ike produced the highly acclaimed *Here and Now* in 2001. He was inducted into the Blues Hall of Fame in 2005. (© David Nester.)

Memphis diva Susan Marshall may not be a household name yet, but anyone who has listened to Lenny Kravitz, the Afghan Whigs, or Lynyrd Skynyrd has heard Marshall's impressive singing chops, a gift that never fails to stop people in their tracks. "Where this woman has been hiding, I don't know," ran a comment on Rockphiles.com. And Rolling Stone made special mention of Marshall's performance at a Gram Parsons tribute that featured Norah Jones, Lucinda Williams, and Keith Richards: "The spine-chill award went to Memphis soul singer Susan Marshall, who belted a powerful 'Do Right Woman' that practically brought people to their knees." (© Steve Roberts.)

Ruby Wilson is the undisputed Queen of Beale Street. She is a Memphis legend who has taken the Delta blues and her powerful, emotional, unforgettable voice worldwide. When she's in Memphis, she's usually holding court at B. B. King's, the epicenter of nightclub entertainment in the mid-South. Ruby has been at the top of her game since arriving in Memphis in 1976. Ruby has appeared in a number of films, such as *Cookie's Fortune*, *The People vs. Larry Flynt*, *The Chamber*, *The Client*, and *The Firm*. (Resource Entertainment Group.)

Willie "Pinetop" Perkins (right) and Kim Wilson pose here at the 2000 Handy Awards. Pinetop has played piano since 1926, when he was just a boy in the Mississippi Delta, and has played with Muddy Waters, Sonny Boy Williamson, and countless others in his long career. He has won more Blues Instrumentalist Handy Awards than anyone. Kim Wilson was a member of the Fabulous Thunderbirds and has been a solo artist since the early 1990s. He won a Handy for Blues Song of the Year in 2004 for "Lookin' for Trouble." (© David Nester.)

At only 21 years old, Daniel "Slick" Ballinger is a rising star in the blues world. He has played with everyone from Pinetop Perkins to Hubert Sumlin and Bob Margolin. He studied at the feet of North Mississippi fife and drum master Othar ("Otha") Turner. Slick has garnered rave reviews for his hard-edged juke joint plus a little gospel style of playing and singing. He wowed the judges and placed second in the 2004 International Blues Challenge sponsored by the Blues Foundation. (Miki Nord.)

Texas bluesman Jimmie Vaughn's 2001 release, *Do You Get the Blues*, was a milestone in his long musical career and was nominated for album of the year in the Handy Awards. Vaughn recorded at Ardent Studios in Memphis and featured blues-great James Cotton on harmonica. (© Steve Roberts.)

Following in the long line of Memphis blues prodigies, Zach Myers has turned a few heads for his straight-ahead blues funk style of guitar playing. He has performed with Buddy Guy, Koko Taylor, ∩ny Wayne Shepherd. The future looks bright for Zach Myers. (© Steve Roberts.)

With Memphis legend Jim Dickinson for a dad and a musical pedigree that reads like fiction, the North Mississippi Allstars are the next generation and natural modern torchbearers for the North Mississippi Hill Country blues tradition begun by the likes of Fred McDowell, Junior Kimbrough, R. L. Burnside, and Othar Turner. As Luther Dickinson says in their Web site biography, "We used to drive down wide eyed and open eared to watch and listen to these giants among men, the kings of the hills playing their music with their people for their people. The musical traditions passing from generation to generation. Down at Otha's we used to boogie in the dirt, dust and gravel. Old ladies teachin' the young girls how to shake 'em on down. The sweaty walls of Jr's Juke Joint used to vibrate and amplify the all night-long moonshine madness. The corn liquor inspired a very unique psychedelic trance blues. The multi-generational musical families gave the old-field hollers a very aggressive loud edge, modern electric country blues." Pictured here from left to right are Chris Chew, Cody Dickinson, and Luther Dickinson. (Photograph by Bob Payne, Red Light Management.)

Clinton, Mississippi, native Billy Gibson first picked up the harmonica at a very young age. "It was cheap and I could easily make sounds with it." After high school, Gibson's desire for learning and improving as a musician took him to Clarksdale, Mississippi, where he played with blues guitarist Johnnie Billington and drummer Bobby Little in Billington's group, the Midnighters. Like many before him, Gibson eventually left Mississippi for Memphis. "Beale Street was my university of blues." (Inside Sounds.)

Brad Webb has been on the Memphis music scene for over 30 years. He is a writer, producer, session musician, and performer. Since 1986, Webb has been producing and performing with Blind Mississippi Morris. (© W. Bearden.)

Another North Mississippi Hill Country blues acolyte, Kenny Brown has performed and recorded with such blues legends as R. L. Burnside and Junior Kimbrough and apprenticed with Johnny Woods and Fred McDowell. Above he is shown on the left with Luther Dickinson and below on the left with R. L. Burnside. His current CD, *Stingray,* has been roundly hailed as a bridge between the past and future of Mississippi juke joint music. (Top and bottom © Steve Roberts.)

Lamar Sorrento's art can be seen in House of Blues locations around the country, on album covers, in art galleries and finer homes. He is also a musician of note and will play blues if you ask him to. He can be seen hard at work painting on his porch in midtown Memphis on most afternoons. Outsider art hardly describes Lamar. At left he is holding his portrait of Robert Johnson. From his self-penned biography from his Web site, "his images are bold and bright and they look good in just about anybody's house. lots of galleries sell his work on al gore's invention (the internet) He also gets tired of writing about himself in the third person. For god's sake, buy some of my art. . . . ok, i know I'm popular because I see artists everywhere who are copying my work. god bless them all. i started all this stuff about 10 years ago—I'm the original. before that i didn't even know how to paint." (© W. Bearden.)

Reba Russell is a Beale Street diva if there ever was one. In the tradition of Koko Taylor and Ma Rainey, she makes a song her own. In addition to producing her own and other artists' albums, Reba's voice has been heard on albums by U2, Tracy Nelson, and Jimmy Thackery. Throughout her career, she has served on boards and committees addressing issues for working musicians. (© Steve Roberts.)

Straight out of the Delta, a bottle-cap encrusted guitar is pictured here. This style of art has become highly collectable in the past few years. The hand-painted, brightly colored, highly adorned indigenous art of the Delta is rarely seen anymore. (© W. Bearden.)

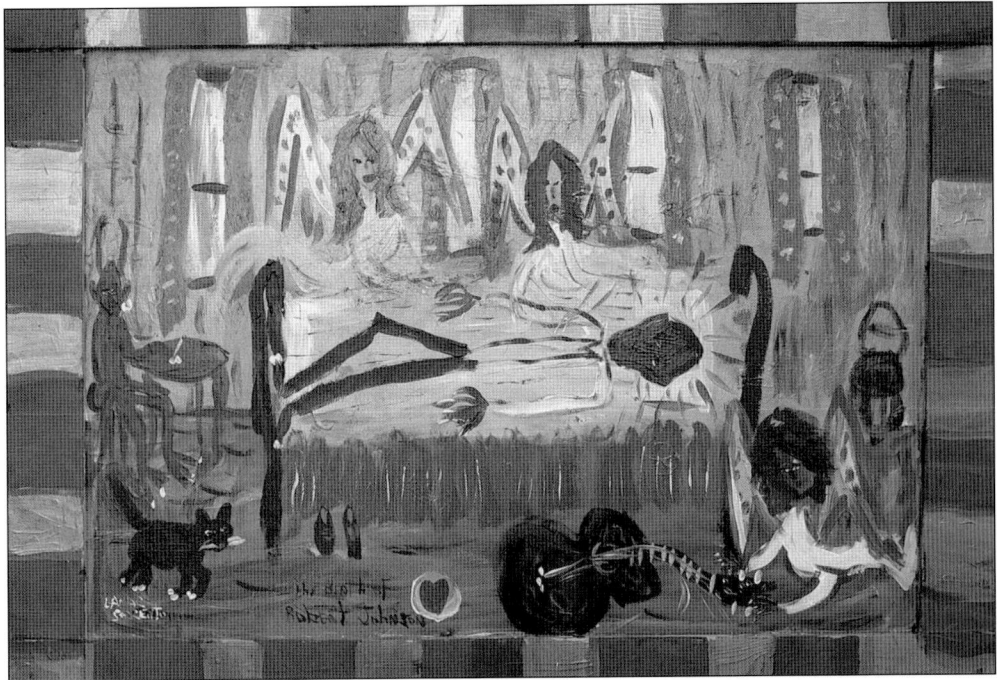

Lamar Sorrento's *Death of Robert Johnson* is a classic in the primitive Delta art genre. Although based in the blues, Sorrento's subjects range from the Beatles to Django Reinhardt, from Johnny Cash to the Who. (Lamar Sorrento.)

Luther (left), Jim (center), and Cody Dickinson perform their brand of Mississippi Hill Country blues. The young Dickinson brothers are, in the author's estimation, fifth-generation practitioners of blues. If the first generation of bluesmen were the great unknowns; the second would be Charley Patton and Son House; the third would have been Muddy Waters, Howlin' Wolf, and the like; the fourth, Eric Clapton, Stevie Ray Vaughn, the Allman Brothers, and that bunch; and the fifth generation, the Dickinsons, Jimbo Mathus, and their contemporaries. (© Steve Roberts.)

Alvin Youngblood Hart is among the new breed of practitioners of the blues. His approach is akin to that of Clarence "Gatemouth" Brown, who defied categorization and simply played the music that moved him. Hart's musical releases have been an eclectic study of a man on a mission. He is one of the most dedicated students of the blues genre yet keeps it fresh and unique by adding his distinctive style. He won Best New Artist at the 1997 Handy Awards. (The Blues Foundation Archive.)

Beale Street Caravan host Pat Mitchell (left) and producer and executive director Sid Selvidge are pictured in the BSC studios on Front Street in Memphis. *Beale Street Caravan* is a monthly, hour-long, internationally syndicated blues show, attracting over two million listeners a week over hundreds of radio stations. Famous blues personalities lend their talents to *Beale Street Caravan*, giving the audience a behind-the-scenes look at blues production and recording, leading them on a historic journey of the blues through exclusive live recordings, and sharing stories of the blues artists themselves. Listeners are treated to special segments by blues industry luminaries such as Grammy-winning producer Bob Porter, noted author Robert Gordon, anthropologist Dick Raichelson, and others. (© W. Bearden.)

Harp King Kim Wilson (right) and Big Jack Johnson (left) jam at the 2001 Handy Awards. Big Jack is a Clarksdale, Mississippi, musician who has traveled widely. In the early 1960s, he teamed up with Frank Frost and Sam Carr to form Frank Frost and the Nighthawks. They later became the Jellyroll Kings and have recorded several albums for Chicago's Earwig Records. (© Bob Sekinger.)

Leo "Tater Red" Allred holds court at his shop on Beale Street, Tater Red's Lucky Mojos, where you can fulfill all of your mojo needs. A native of Ruleville in the Mississippi Delta, Tater Red has the distinction of hosting the longest-running blues show on Memphis radio. The shop is a must-see place on Beale, filled to the rafters with interesting gifts and clothing—all with a blues flair. Tater Red is also widely known for his original art. His "Blues Shrines" and other Delta-influenced pieces of art are highly coveted. A case can be made that Tater Red is the Mayor of Beale Street. (© W. Bearden.)

Tater Red is shown here with ZZ Top guitarist Billy Gibbons. The shop on Beale is a frequent stop for celebrities of every stripe. (Tater Red.)

If you visit Tater Red's, notice the autographed drumheads on the ceiling. Bumper stickers, buttons, posters, t-shirts, jackets, voodoo dolls, candles, and oils can be found in the store. His homemade labels on the hex-removing oils are worth a visit by themselves. "Other Lawyer Be Stupid," "Boss Ease Off," and "Do As I Say" are some favorites. (Tater Red.)

Who's that with Tater Red? In this case, it's Warren Haynes (left) and Allen Woody (right) of Gov't. Mule. Haynes and Woody performed with Little Milton at the 2000 Handy Awards show in Memphis. Their work in Gov't. Mule and the Allman Brothers Band was some of the finest in recent history. Woody passed away in August 2000. (© W. Bearden.)

Junior Wells (center) poses with Tater Red. Wells, whose given name was Amos Blackmore, was born and raised in West Memphis, Arkansas. He moved with his mother to Chicago in the mid-1940s and quickly gained a reputation for being a master of the blues harmonica. He played with Muddy Waters for a time and went on to have a long and successful career. His "Hoo Doo Man," "Blues Hit Big Town," and "Messin' With the Kid" are required listening. He died in Chicago in 1998. (Tater Red.)

Memphis music royalty David Porter (left), Knox Phillips (center), and Isaac Hayes are shown here. The team of Hayes and Porter are responsible for more hits than any other soul music songwriters. The hits are endless: "Soul Man," "Hold On I'm Comin'," "Shaft," and on and on. As a producer, Knox has worked with artists as diverse as Etta James and John Prine. (© Steve Roberts.)

On re-opening day of Earnestine and Hazel's, a former café and hotel on Memphis's South Main Street, singer Larry Springfield (left) gets ready for a performance. The club is a popular spot for the many residents who live in the downtown area of Memphis. (© Steve Roberts.)

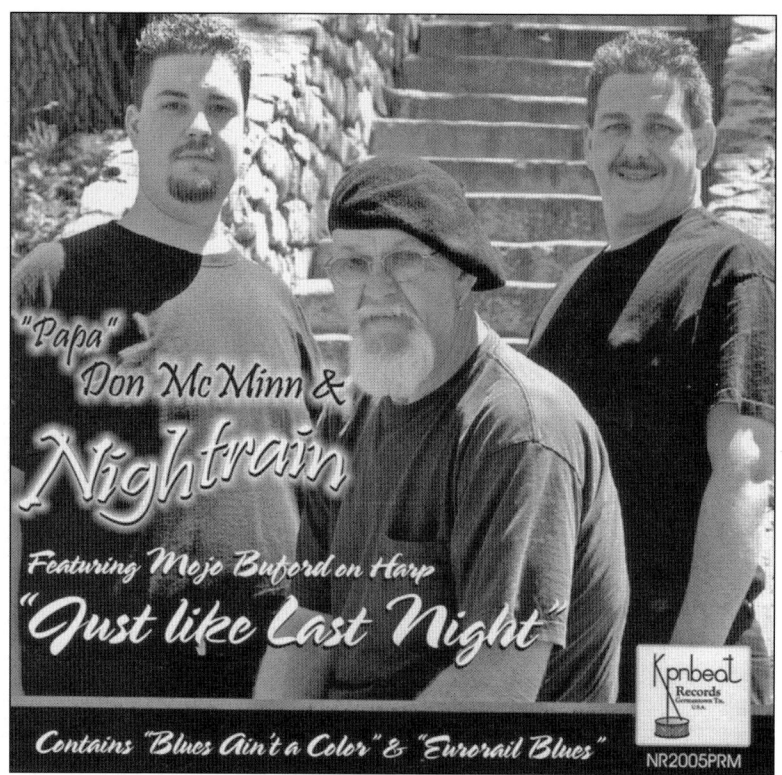

Memphis blues legend Don McMinn and sons Rome (left) and Doug have been a fixture on the Memphis music scene for many years. Don and the boys helped kick-start the rebirth of Beale Street by serving as the house band at the Rum Boogie Café. They regularly tour North America and Europe, spreading the blues around the world. The band's latest release is *Just like Last Night*. (Doug McMinn.)

Booker T. Jones (left) and Steve Cropper are shown here in front of the Memphis skyline. The longtime partners in Booker T and the MG's are legends in Memphis and around the world. Their partnership is the greatest testament to the Memphis magic—black and white are bonded together in the love of music. (© Steve Roberts.)

Co-founder and executive producer of the Center for Southern Folklore, Judy Peiser has been one of the chief advocates for Memphis music for over 40 years. The center's mission is "to preserve, defend and promote the music, culture, arts, and rhythms of the South. The goal is to develop programs in the print and broadcast media, cyberspace, public performance venues, tourism and education that celebrate the region's cultural heritage." The center, which is located at 119 South Main Street, features a café and performance space where authentic blues, jazz, soul, and rockabilly can be heard. The annual Memphis Music and Heritage Festival, held each Labor Day weekend, is a Memphis favorite. (© W. Bearden.)

The blues and rock 'n roll mecca, Sun Studios, at 706 Union Avenue, is pictured here. In this small studio, Sam Phillips recorded his seminal records with B. B. King, Howlin' Wolf, Rufus Thomas, Roscoe Gordon, Elvis Presley, Carl Perkins, Johnny Cash, Roy Orbison, and Jerry Lee Lewis. Here he changed the world. (© W. Bearden.)

The highway beckons blues lovers from the world over. Highways 61 and 49 are the mythical "crossroads" where Robert Johnson is said to have sold his soul to the Devil. More accurately, these highways were the arteries out of the Delta for hundreds of thousands of African Americans who moved north, looking for better times and more opportunity. These truly are the blues highways. (© W. Bearden.)

SUGGESTED READING

Below is an informal, unscientific, and off-the-cuff list of books to read if you're interested in learning more about the blues and the Memphis music scene, past and present. These books have both illuminated and inspired me and pushed along my search for the essence of what we are as Southerners. I hope you will enjoy and share the wonderful stories told here.

Booth, Stanley. *Rhythm Oil*. New York, NY: Pantheon, 2000.

Edwards, David "Honeyboy." *The World Don't Owe Me Nothin'*. Chicago, IL: Chicago Review Press, 2000.

Ferris, William. *Blues From The Delta*. New York, NY: Doubleday, 1978.

Gordon, Robert and Bruce Nemerov, eds. *Lost Delta Found*. Nashville: Vanderbilt UP, 2005.

———. *It Came From Memphis*. New York, NY: Faber and Faber, 1995.

———. *Can't Be Satisfied, The Life and Times of Muddy Waters*. New York, NY: Little, Brown, 2002.

Guralnick, Peter. *Sweet Soul Music*. New York, NY: Little, Brown, 1986.

———. *Searching for Robert Johnson*. New York, NY: Penguin, 1989.

Lomax, Alan. *The Land Where Blues Began*. New York, NY: Pantheon, 1993.

Nix, Don. *Road Stories and Recipes*. New York, NY: Shirmer Books, 1997.

Oakley, Giles. *The Devil's Music: A History of the Blues*. New York, NY: Taplinger, 1977.

Palmer, Robert. *Deep Blues*. New York, NY: Viking Press, 1981.

This is sure to get me in trouble, but I'm going to suggest some of my favorite blues music should you feel compelled to further your study and enjoyment of the blues. A more complete list would take several pages and incite much controversy, so I'm offering an eclectic mix (actually, what I can readily see in my record collection) of what has moved me in some physical way, made me smile, or made me think a little deeper.

Allison, Mose. *Your Mind is on Vacation*. Koch Records, 2000, Audio CD.

Dickinson, James Luther. *Dixie Fried*. Sepia Tone Records, 2002, Audio CD.

Hurt, Mississippi John. *The Best of Mississippi John Hurt*. Vanguard Records, 1990, Audio CD.

King B. B. *Indianola Mississippi Seeds*. MCA Records, 1989, Audio CD.

King, Albert. *I'll Play the Blues For You*. Stax Records, 1990, Audio CD.

King, Freddie. *Getting Ready*. The Right Stuff, 1996, Audio CD.

Lewis, Furry. *Take Your Time*. Gene's Records, 1999, Audio CD.

McDowell, Fred. *I Do Not Play No Rock and Roll*. Varese Records, 2001, Audio CD.

Memphis Jug Band. *The Best of the Memphis Jug Band*. Yazoo Records, 2001, Audio CD.

Nix, Don. *Going Down: the Songs of Don Nix*. Evidence Records, 2002, Audio CD.

Reed, Jimmy. *The Best of Jimmy Reed*. GNP Crescendo, 2000, Audio CD.

Selvidge, Sid. *The Cold of the Morning*. Archer-records.com, 2003, Audio CD.

Selvidge, Sid. *A Little Bit of Rain*. Archer-records.com, 2003, Audio CD.

Selvidge, Sid. *Live At Otherlands*. Archer-records.com, 2005, Audio CD and DVD with interviews.

Slim, Memphis. *Blue Memphis*. Wounded Bird Records, 2005, Audio CD.

Turner, Otha. *Everybody Hollerin' Goat*. Birdman Records, 1998, Audio CD.

Various Artists. *Beale Street Saturday Night, Various Artists, Produced by Jim Dickinson*. Memphis Development Foundation, 1979, LP.

Vaughn, Jimmy. *Do You Get the Blues?* Artemis Records, 2001, Audio CD.

Waters, Muddy. *Electric Mud*. Chess Records, 1996, Audio CD.

———. *Folk Singer*. Chess Records, 1999, Audio CD.

———. *Hard Again*. Sony Records, 2004, Audio CD.

———. *The Plantation Recordings*. Chess Records, 1993, Audio CD.

Wells, Junior. *Hoo Doo Man Blues*. Delmark Records, 1993, Audio CD.

Wolf, Howlin'. *His Best*. Chess Records, 1997, Audio CD.